Portugal
A Land of Fun in the Sun

PEDRO PEREIRA
CHRISTINA KRONBACK

Copyright © 2023 Pedro Pereira Christina Kronback
All rights reserved.
ISBN: 9798374545357

DEDICATION

To our daughters Marie Louise and Anne Sophie

This book belongs to
_ _ _ _ _ _ _ _ _ _ _ _ _ _ _

Portugal

Once upon a time, in a land far, far away, there was a beautiful country called Portugal. Portugal was known for its warm sunshine, delicious seafood, and friendly people.

The biggest city in Portugal was Lisbon, which was built on seven hills. Lisbon was famous for its colourful houses, trams, and beautiful streets. The city was also known for its delicious pastry the famous Pastel de Nata.

Portugal was also home to many beautiful beaches from North to South. Children loved to play in the sand and swim in the ocean. They also enjoyed collecting seashells and watching the waves roll in.

In the countryside of Portugal, there were many vineyards and olive groves. The people of Portugal made delicious wine and olive oil from the grapes and olives. They also grew many different kinds of fruits and vegetables, such as oranges, lemons, and tomatoes.

One of the most famous landmarks in Portugal was the Tower of Belém. It was built a very long time ago and was a symbol of Portugal's great age of exploration. Many famous explorers, such as Vasco da Gama, set sail from the Tower of Belém to discover new lands.

But that's not all, there were many more pretty castles and big palaces all over Portugal. From the city of Guimarães to the region of Algarve, you can find them everywhere! We can even imagine ourselves as princesses and princes living in those castles.

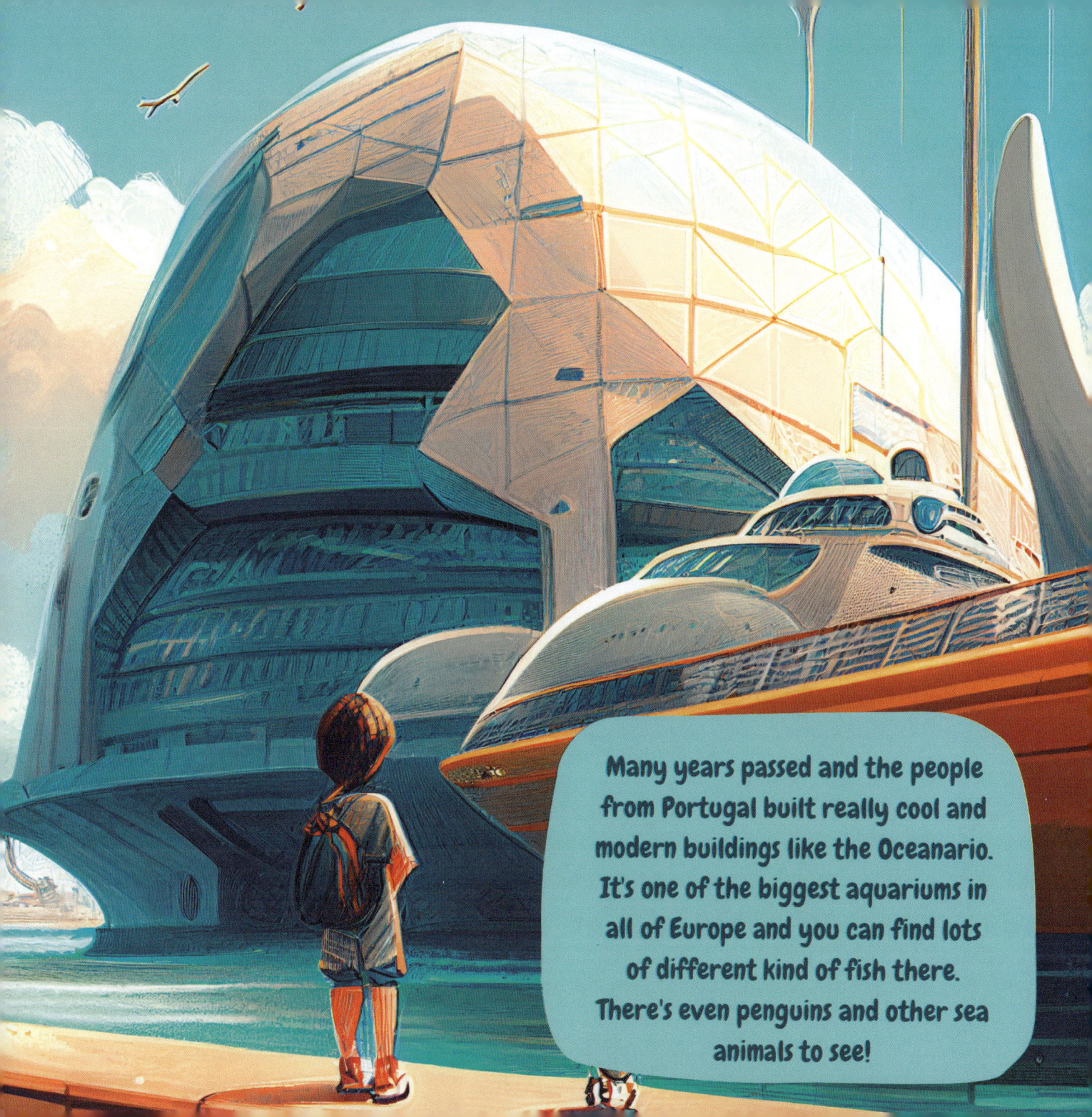

Many years passed and the people from Portugal built really cool and modern buildings like the Oceanario. It's one of the biggest aquariums in all of Europe and you can find lots of different kind of fish there. There's even penguins and other sea animals to see!

The Portuguese are very proud of their country and its history. They love to share their culture and traditions with visitors from all over the world. If you ever have a chance to visit Portugal, you will be sure to have a wonderful time!

The End

More about Portugal

EASY TO SAY WORDS

- OLÁ (OH-LAH) - HELLO
- OBRIGADO (O-BREE-GA-DOO) - THANKS
- ADEUS (A-DEH-OOSH) - GOODBYE
- SIM (SANG) - YES
- NÃO (NOW) - NO
- POR FAVOR (POR FAH-VOHR) - PLEASE
- DESCULPE (DEH-SKOL-PEH) - I'M SORRY

PLACES TO VISIT

- **OCEANARIO DE LISBOA:** THE LARGEST INDOOR AQUARIUM IN EUROPE, WHERE CHILDREN CAN SEE A WIDE VARIETY OF SEA CREATURES, INCLUDING SHARKS, RAYS AND SEAHORSES.

- **PALÁCIO NACIONAL DE SINTRA:** A PALACE LOCATED IN SINTRA, WHERE CHILDREN CAN LEARN ABOUT THE HISTORY OF PORTUGAL AND SEE BEAUTIFUL PALACES AND GARDENS.

- **ZOOMARINE:** AN MARINE-LIFE PARK LOCATED IN THE ALGARVE, WHERE CHILDREN CAN SEE DOLPHINS AND SEA LIONS SHOWS, AS WELL AS A VARIETY OF ANIMALS AND BIRDS.

- **CHOCOLATE MUSEUM:** A FUN AND INTERACTIVE MUSEUM IN PORTO, WHERE CHILDREN CAN LEARN ABOUT THE HISTORY OF CHOCOLATE AND EVEN MAKE THEIR OWN CHOCOLATE.

- **FÁBRICA DE NATAL DA LAGOA:** A CHRISTMAS-THEMED PARK LOCATED IN THE AZORES, WHERE CHILDREN CAN VISIT SANTA'S WORKSHOP, AND SEE CHRISTMAS LIGHTS AND DECORATIONS.

MAKE YOUR OWN PASTEL DE NATA!

INGREDIENTS
- 1 CUP OF FLOUR
- 2 EGGS
- 1/2 CUP OF SUGAR
- 1/4 CUP OF BUTTER
- 1/4 CUP OF CREAM

INSTRUCTIONS:

OKAY KIDDO, WE'RE GOING TO MAKE A YUMMY TREAT CALLED PASTEL DE NATA! IT'S A TYPE OF PASTRY THAT IS VERY POPULAR IN PORTUGAL.

FIRST, WE WILL NEED SOME INGREDIENTS LIKE FLOUR, EGGS, SUGAR, BUTTER, AND CREAM.

NEXT, WE WILL MIX THE FLOUR AND EGGS TOGETHER TO MAKE A DOUGH. THEN, WE WILL ROLL OUT THE DOUGH AND CUT IT INTO SMALL CIRCLES.

NEXT, WE WILL PUT SOME BUTTER, SUGAR AND CREAM IN A PAN AND COOK IT UNTIL IT BECOMES NICE AND THICK.

THEN WE WILL PUT THE DOUGH CIRCLES INTO THE CUPS OF A CUPCAKE PAN AND POUR THE MIXTURE OF SUGAR, BUTTER AND CREAM ON TOP.

FINALLY, WE'LL PUT IT IN THE OVEN AND BAKE IT UNTIL IT BECOMES GOLDEN BROWN AND CRISPY.
WHEN IT'S DONE, WE CAN TAKE IT OUT OF THE OVEN AND LET IT COOL FOR A BIT. THEN WE CAN ENJOY OUR YUMMY PASTEL DE NATA!
IT'S A BIT HARD TO MAKE, BUT IT'S WORTH IT BECAUSE IT'S DELICIOUS!

Diary

Use this page for the pictures of your first trip to Portugal..

Colouring Portugal

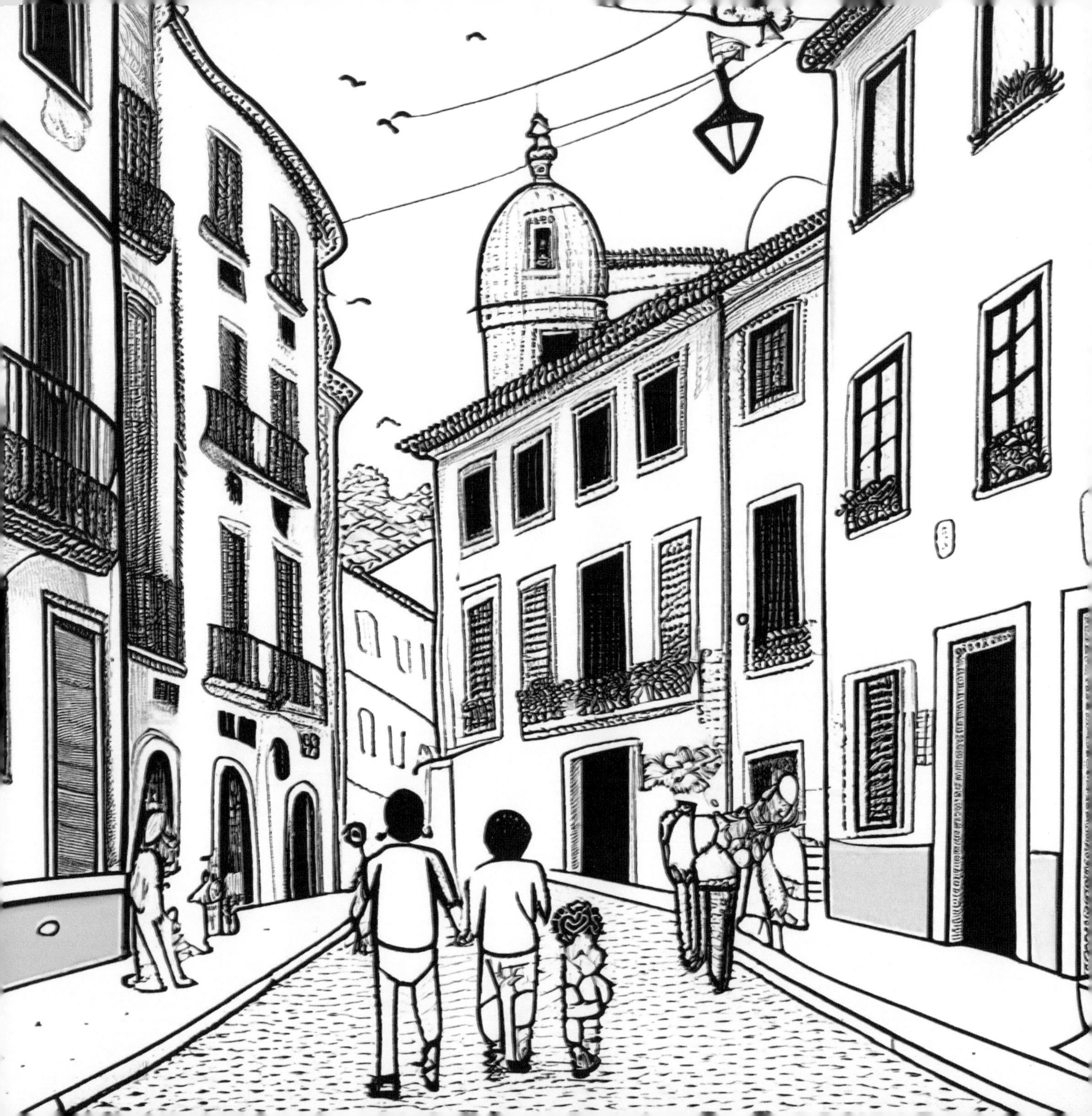

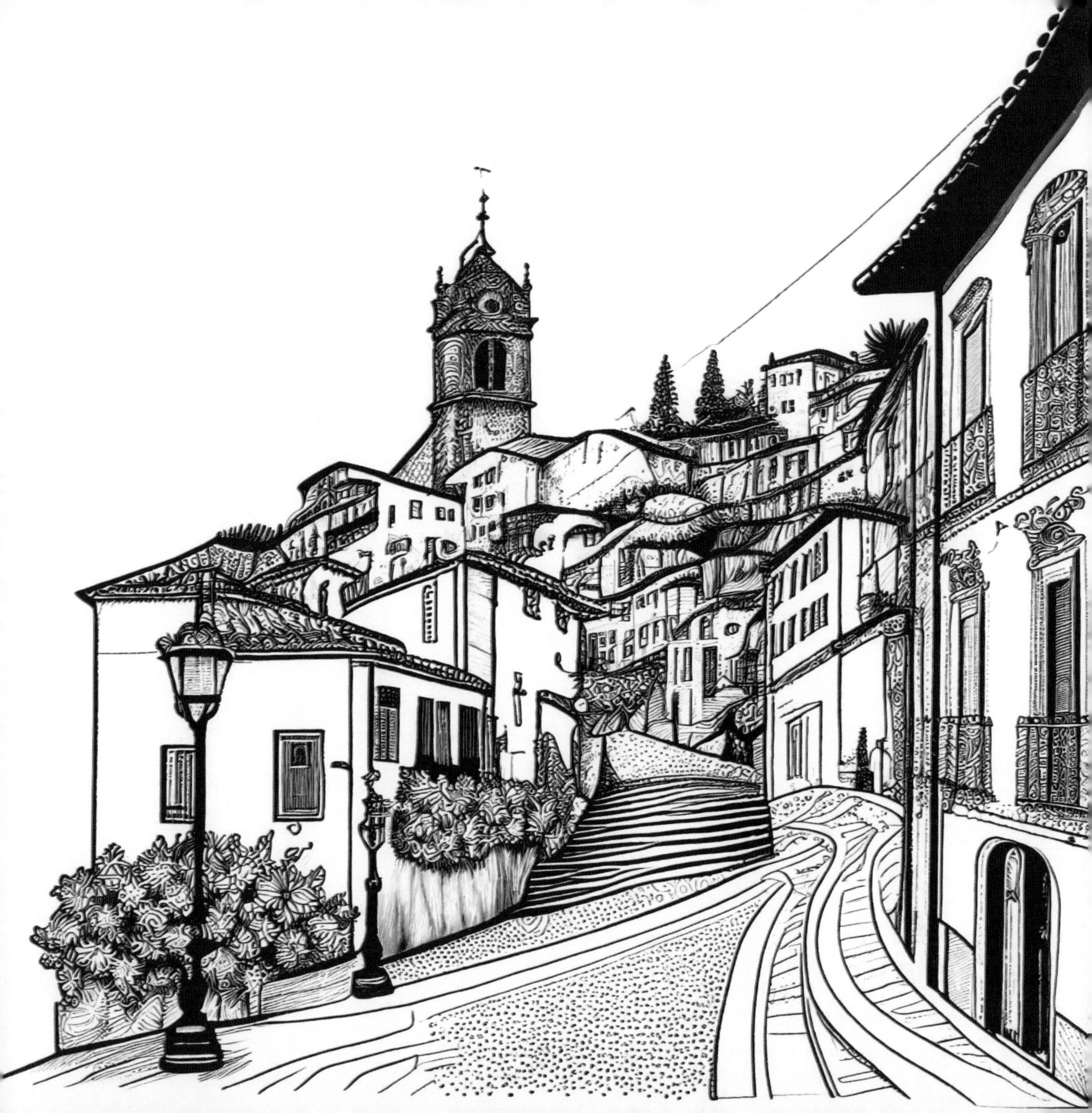

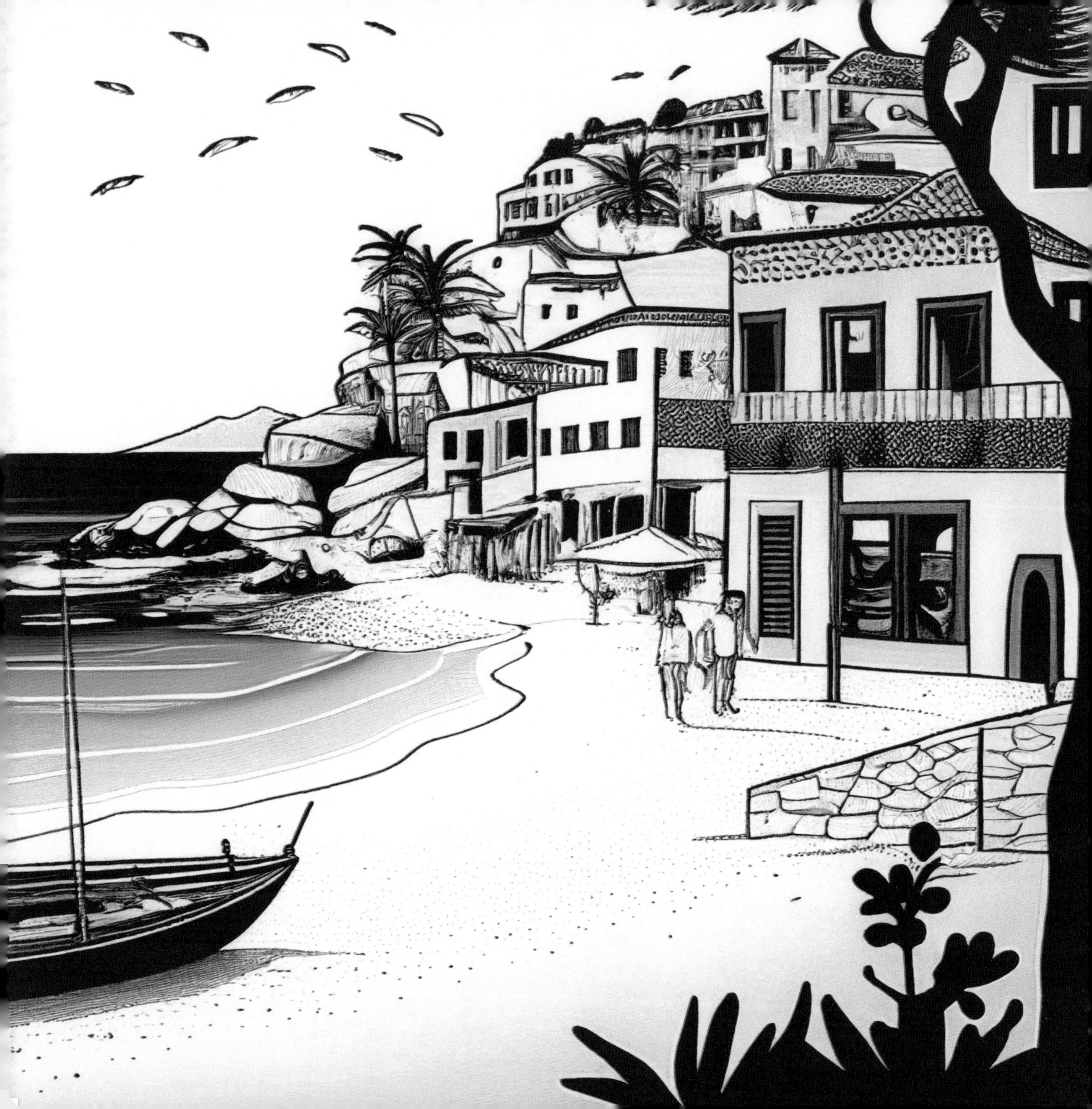

Printed in Great Britain
by Amazon

Quick & Easy Vegetarian Curry Recipes

That Taste Amazing!

Julian Voigt

© Julian Voigt 2015 all rights reserved

This publication is published by the author

No part of this book may be reproduced copied or turned into audio without the author's expressed consent

For more recipes and cooking tips visit: www.curryrecipesecrets.com
You can contact the author at: julianvoigt_23@hotmail.com

Table of Contents

Why I Wrote This Recipe Book 1

Why YOU Should Read This Book 4

How This Book Works 6

Key Conventions, Measures, and Conversions 9

Why Go Veggie? 11

Consider Your Health 13

A Worrying Statistic 15

Some Veggie Facts 17

The Economics 19

Consider the Animals 20

Consider the Planet 21

Spices We Will Be Using and Where You Might Find Them 23

    Black Mustard Seeds 24

    Fenugreek Seeds 24

    Cumin Seeds (Brown) 24

    Large Dried Red Chillies (Kashmiri Type) 25

    Cinnamon Stick 25

    Asafoetida (a.k.a. Hing) 25

    Green Cardamom 25

    Curry Leaves 26

    Cloves 26

    Methi Leaves 26

    Panch Phoran 27

    Kokum 27

Powdered Spices You Will Need 28

    Deggi Mirch (Deep Red Chilli Powder) 28

    Turmeric 28

    Coriander 28

    Cumin 29

Spice Blends (Masalas) 31

    Chaat Masala 31

    Garam Masala 31

    Tandoori Masala 32

Online Stores That Sell Spices and South Asian Foodstuffs 33

The 'Oh So Hallowed Dal' 35

Recipes—Let's Get Cooking! 44

Gujarati Dal 45

Bengali Egg Curry 48

Cauliflower & Pea Curry 51

Dal Toori 54

Khadi (Hot Yoghurt Soup) 57

Punjabi Dal Fry 60

Cabbage Curry (VV) 63

Rajma (VV) 66

Aubergine & Peanut Curry (VV) 69

Potato Curry 72

Channa Dal (VV) 75

Mung Bean Curried Stew (VV) 78

Mixed Vegetable Tikka Masala (VV) 81

Butter Paneer 84

Tomato & Potato Curry (VV) 86

Split Mung Dal with Spinach (VV) 89

About the Author 97

Why I Wrote This Recipe Book

Vegetarian food is a subject close to my heart and one I feel passionate about. My other passion in life is curry—put the two together and we have vegetarian Indian cuisine. I have chosen to feature the authentic version as eaten by people in India.

This is not just a curry recipe book about vegetarian dishes; the recipes that I have chosen to include in this book had to accomplish three things: 1) be **quick** to make, 2) be **easy** to make, and 3) be incredibly **tasty**! Hence, you will note that most of the recipes in this book can be prepared and cooked in 20 minutes or less!

Different recipe books accomplish different things. My vision for this book was to give you recipe insights and techniques that would enable you to put a curry on the table that took less than 30 minutes to make but tasted like it had been cooked for hours.

Another requirement for this book was that most of the recipes had to be simple to make and require the bare minimum of ingredients. Is this a gimmick? No! Many dishes in India are cooked this way because the reality is that most people are poor, and they have limited cooking facilities. Yet, out of those very basic and limited circumstances have evolved some of the most sublime dishes the world has ever seen!

As I have already mentioned, vegetarian curry cooking is a subject that is close to my heart, as I am a vegetarian. In this book, I'm going to give you some compelling reasons why you should make more vegetarian choices in your diet. Don't worry, I'm not going to start waving the vegetarian banner. Yet, I do believe it's in everyone's best interests to add more plant-based foods to their diet and cut out, or at least cut back, on meat. Here is an interesting fact for you: South Asian cuisine has **the** most varied vegetarian cuisine, bar none.

In fact, as I have mentioned in my other recipe books, *Indian* cuisine, as most people know it, particularly here in the UK, is actually a far cry from what *real* Indian, or should we say South Asian cuisine is all about.

Here is a fact many people are not aware of: India has the lowest rate of meat consumption in the world; yet, most people visiting a so-called Indian restaurant here in the UK often see that the dishes on the menu revolve around chicken, lamb, or king prawn. Hence, dishes like Chicken Tikka Masala and Lamb Bhuna (you get the idea).

Sadly, the vegetable options in many Indian restaurants are nothing more than an afterthought—you know, the so-called *side* dishes. *I'm sure you understand where I'm coming from here!* To add insult to injury, many of those so-called side dishes are cooked with frozen vegetables! To me this is a real shame because South Asian cuisine has **the** most varied vegetarian cuisine going, not to mention the tastiest.

I'm convinced (and you'll probably say I'm biased) that if Indian restaurants were to add **real** Indian vegetarian fare to their menu—the type eaten my most people in India and no doubt by the staff that work in those establishments—then I am convinced we would all soon ditch the Chicken Tikka Masala in favour of a sumptuous Baingan Bharta.

There is another compelling reason to consider *real* Indian vegetarian cuisine and it's this: ***it's easy***! You will not need any base gravy, marinades, pastes, or potions for this style of cooking, nor do these recipes have a huge ingredients list either. In fact, some of the tastiest veggie dishes have but one vegetable. Most of the recipes in this book can also be prepared and on your table in 20 minutes. Oh, and by the way, in case I haven't already mentioned it— ***they taste incredible too***!

Why YOU Should Read This Book

It doesn't matter whether you are a vegetarian, vegan, or omnivore, everyone can benefit from the ideas I put forward in this book, not to mention the recipes (it is a recipe book after all!).

We are living in a time when there is an abundance of information as well as evidence to prove that eating a more plant-centred diet is the healthy thing to do.

The problem lies in the fact that, while there may be an abundance of information and evidence to suggest we consume more fruits, vegetables, and legumes, we are also living in a time when we are busier than ever and, at the same time, *conveniently* surrounded by a vast choice of processed food and readymade meals. In turn, this has fostered a *food illiteracy*—to coin a phrase—in that we are losing our knowledge of foods and how to prepare them. We have inadvertently subcontracted out our responsibility to care for our *own* diet to huge food companies who are more than happy to take on that responsibility.

In my humble opinion, we need to re-educate ourselves and take back the responsibility to be more mindful with regard to what we allow into our mouths. The problem remains, however, that many of us are living pressured lives, and we find ourselves limited when it comes to the time we can spend making something that is tasty and, at the same time, nutritious.

This is why I decided to write this book and provide you with know-how and recipes that tick all three boxes: 1. food that is healthy and nutritious, 2. tasty (*if it don't taste good we won't eat it!*), and 3. quick to make.

In my opinion (and I am biased), curry is the world's tastiest food, bar none. When I say *curry,* what I really mean is South Asian cuisine and that includes food from India, Bangladesh, and Pakistan.

My hope is that after reading this book and trying out the recipes, you'll agree with me that there are **no more excuses**!

How This Book Works

With regard to the recipes in this book, you will find a brief description about the recipe, the estimated preparation and cook time, and how many people the recipe serves.

After the description, you will find a list of ingredients followed by the cooking method, followed by the **Chef's Notes**. These notes are there to give you that little something extra to help you get the most out of the dish or perhaps reveal a trick or tip.

In my previous books, there are links to videos that complement the recipes in the books and these are a feature that many have found a great help, as you actually see someone cooking the dish. However, as I have decided to make all my future books available in print form as well as in eBook format, I have decided to leave the video links (URLs) out of the text, as this obviously does not work with the printed version of the book.

Hence, it was decided that I would produce the videos separately and make these available on my YouTube channel for you to access as and when you need them.

The videos will not all appear at once but in a sequence over time and will be referenced and found through the search bar on my YouTube channel. For example, you can search for: *Quick & Easy Gujarati Dal.* In other words, the recipe prefixed by the words *'Quick & Easy.'*

Another reason for the change was that when writing a recipe book and simultaneously creating videos to accompany those recipes, mistakes happened because we were working to a deadline. There have been quite a few variations between the written recipe and the video version of that recipe, which has led to confusion on the part of the reader and a ton of emails directed my way to clarify the matter. Hence, it seemed a much better idea to concentrate first and foremost on the book and make sure that it was as good as it could be and then, after the book was completed, to start work on the video versions of the recipes in the book. *In doing so, I could make sure that I stayed faithful to the written recipe!* ☺

Hopefully, by the time you read this, there should be at least some videos completed to complement the recipes in this book. The videos will not be locked and will be viewable to the public. You can find my YouTube channel by searching YouTube with my name: Julian Voigt.

In this book, many of the dishes are based on authentic regional dishes from India, exploring various ingredients, cooking style, and flavours.

Generally speaking, curries in India are based around three different bases or gravies. For example, you have dishes made with an onion-based gravy—this is where they use copious amounts of onion cooked till brown to add a depth of flavour to a dish.

Then there are the tomato-based curries where the flavour in the dish comes predominantly from tomatoes, which are plentiful in India. Then there are those delicious yoghurt-based curries that are creamy but with that distinctive tang.

Once you have learned to make these various sauces, then the world is your oyster and you can now go on to create many varied and fantastic dishes of your own using different variations of spices and using different vegetables, beans, and dals.

Opportunity!

If you have come up with a tasty recipe and think other people would like it too, then send me the recipe.

I will make this recipe, feature it on my YouTube channel, and give you a 'shout out' and thanks for sharing the recipe. I may even feature the recipe in one of my future books (with due credit given to you of course).

Also, any recipes that I try and think are good enough to get featured, the contributor of that recipe will receive a FREE signed printed copy of any one of my books (they choose) as a thank you.

Send your recipe to: julianvoigt_23@hotmail.com

Okay, back to the book. Now, before we go any further, I'm going to give you the key conventions and measurements used in this book as well as some abbreviations I use.

Key Conventions, Measures, and Conversions

I have tried to consistently standardise the way information is presented, and you will note that the recipes start with the amount followed by the ingredients.

TBSP v tsp—to avoid confusion Tablespoon = TBSP in UPPERCASE
Whereas teaspoon = tsp in lower case

To indicate a heaped tablespoon = H/TBSP
To indicate a heaped teaspoon = h/tsp

1 TBSP = 17 ml
1 tsp = 6 ml
Chef's Spoon = 30 g
Cup = 250 ml

'A pinch' simply refers to the small amount of spice that you can hold between your thumb and forefinger.

If in doubt, the rule of thumb is go with less rather than more as you can always add it, but you can't subtract it.

Terms like 'Indian' and 'curry' are used in a general sense as applied to foods from all of South Asia.

Now that you have those terms, you should be able to make sense of the recipes that will follow. And, talking of recipes, you might be wondering why I decided to write a book all about vegetarian Indian food. In the next section of this book, I will answer that question.

Why Go Veggie?

Well, I could write a book on this subject alone, but I will refrain myself here and give you what I consider the most compelling reasons to cook vegetarian. Don't worry, I'm not preaching vegetarianism, everyone can enjoy this style of cooking—vegan, vegetarian, flexitarian, and meat eater alike.

My own personal journey towards a vegetarian diet took many years and was motivated by a desire for better health and weight loss rather than for ethical reasons. Don't get me wrong, I love animals but, essentially, my original motivation was a selfish one.

Often people look at a vegetarian diet as one that will deprive them of certain foods they love. I see it differently.

I see the transition to a plant-based diet as a diet of more variety and an exploration of *other* foods. In the past, although meat was the main item on my plate, I was actually excluding *other* foods. It is possible a meat-based diet *could* be a diet of deprivation in that by making meat the main ingredient in our meal, we inadvertently deprive ourselves of many other *more* nutritious foods that find no room on our plate, if you get where I'm coming from.

This subject, amongst others, will be discussed on my new YouTube channel, 'You are what you eat.' So, look out for that.

In this book, all the recipes here are vegetarian and many are also vegan. The difference between vegetarian and vegan is that vegans do not consume any animal products whatsoever—no milk or milk derived products, which would include cream, yoghurt, butter, and ghee. Vegans do not eat eggs either. In this book, if you see a recipe with a double v = VV, then the recipe is vegan. In some instances, yoghurt can be replaced with a soya yoghurt or coconut yoghurt. Cream can be replaced by soya cream.

Consider Your Health

The old adage, 'you are what you eat,' is universally accepted and understood and now more than ever we know the importance of good nutrition and its connection to our health.

"A diet rich in fruits and vegetables plays a role in reducing the risk of all the major causes of illness and death," **says Walter Willett, chair of the nutrition department at the Harvard School of Public Health.**

As the quote above states, a plant-based diet has been proven scientifically to be the best *health* promoting diet of all. When we look at populations of people around the world that consume a mostly plant-based diet, what do we see? We see this: not only do they live longer, but they don't suffer with the plethora of diseases that we do in the West. The aptly named SAD diet (standard American diet) with its emphasis on meat and dairy and processed foods has long been linked to preventable diseases like diabetes, heart disease, and even cancer, not to mention obesity.

How often are we reminded to make sure we get our 5 a day? Maybe you too should include more plant foods in your diet.

Often, the reasons given why people do not eat more plant-based foods is because they either don't taste very nice or they're not sure how to make a tasty meal with *just* vegetables.

My hope is that this book will both dispel any doubts that vegetable dishes can't taste amazing—because they can—and I'm going to be so bold as to assert that, in most cases, they even taste *better* than their meat counterparts. So, no more excuses!

By dispelling the myth that vegetable-based dishes are not as tasty as their meat counterparts, I will show you just how *easy* it is to make delicious and exciting meals that don't have any meat in them. In fact, I'm convinced that if you're not already into cooking vegetarian-style curries, after reading this book and cooking some of the recipes in it, you'll be choosing them over your meat-based options from now on.

Have you also noticed that in countries where people consume a more plant-based diet, they are often leaner than many of us are here? In countries like India and China most people are nice and slim.

I think the fact that they're eating a more plant-centred diet has a large bearing on that. So, if you're looking to shed a few kilos, then eating more plant-based foods will bring added bonuses.

A Worrying Statistic

I was shocked to learn that here in the UK we, on average, consume around 40% of our total calories from fat and much of that is animal-based saturated fat. No wonder many of us are struggling to keep our waistlines in check.

It's not only meat and dairy that are to blame, but it's also all the refined carbohydrates and processed food we are eating that adds to the problem.

For those of you who follow my YouTube channel, 'Curry Secrets,' you may be aware from a video I made entitled 'What's Happening?' that about four years ago, after struggling with some health issues for most of my life, I made some dietary changes.

These changes had a *hugely* positive effect on my health. What were those changes? Well, basically, I changed my diet from eating a lot of meat and processed foods to a plant-based diet. I didn't go all out vegetarian overnight; I just started including more vegetables and eating less meat. I also supercharged my veggie intake by adopting the daily habit of juicing, and that one change alone made a huge difference, but I will save that subject for another time. Having cut out all of the processed junk food, I lost weight and, at the same time, my energy levels soared.

It was over about an eighteen-month period that I went from 15 stone (95 kg) to 11 stone (70 kg). My blood pressure came down (*it had been high for quite a while*) and a peptic stomach, that had blighted my life for twenty years, healed.

'Wow!' I thought. If I had known about this stuff earlier, I would have made these changes sooner.

Did I feel like I was depriving myself by making these changes? No! In fact, the way I looked at it was this: 'Look at all these great *new* foods that I'm adding to my diet.' They were delicious and interesting foods that I had been depriving myself of for many years.

I think this way of looking at it is a much more *empowering* mind-set because you know as well as I do that whenever we tell ourselves that we *can't* have something, guess what happens? We want it all the more! This is the number one reason why diets don't work!

I found that by eating a more plant-based diet that, firstly, I could eat all I cared for without putting the weight back on (*no small portions here*) and, secondly, I felt better! You see, vegetables, fruits, and legumes are mostly carbohydrate calorie sources. So, by eating more of these types of foods, you automatically reduce the fat levels in your diet without having to even think about it. You just have to be careful not to add too much oil to your dishes, but more about that later in the recipes section of this book.

As a thank you for buying this book, head over to my website and sign up. You will receive a FREE curry recipes eBook, and my regular newsletter with lots of tips, tricks, and recipes. www.curryrecipesecrets.com ☺

Some Veggie Facts

1. Fruits and vegetables contain something that meat and dairy products don't—fibre! Guess what? Fibre not only keeps you regular but also gives you the sensation of being full, hence you tend not to overeat with fibre-rich foods.

2. Fruits, vegetables, and legumes are naturally low in fat.

3. Legumes (chickpeas, lentils, and pulses) are protein rich foods, and they make a great meat replacement. They'll also keep you feeling fuller longer.

4. Eating a more plant-based diet is less expensive than a meat-based one.

5. Dried foods like lentils, beans, and pulses can be bought in bulk inexpensively, and they keep for months.

6. Plant-based foods are less of a challenge for your digestive system.

7. Cultures that eat a predominantly plant-based diet live longer. Check out the Okinawans.

8. High meat consumption has been linked with bowel cancer. Guess which country has one of the lowest incidences of bowel cancer? You guessed it—India.

9. Eating more plant-based foods helps you look younger.

10. Eating more plant-based foods gives you more energy.

The Economics

$ £ €

'Fewer cows and fatter hogs are behind rises in the price of meat....' according to the *Guardian* newspaper. Meat prices are set to increase yet again. As the demand for meat rises, the supply struggles to keep up with the demand.

Choosing to eat more plant-based meals is definitely easier on the pocket and, you never know, you might take some of that cash you save and spend it on a new gym membership. Who knows how far this thing might go or what extremes you might go to....

Consider the Animals

I'm sure those chickens, sheep, cows, and pigs would thank us for choosing *not* to eat them. Let's face it, most of us couldn't slaughter our own animals. I know I couldn't. We prefer to let someone else do that for us. I'm convinced that if we had to spend an afternoon in a slaughter house we might come out of there feeling a lot more inclined to choose veggie meals over meat ones.

As the demand for meat rises along with the planet's population, it's safe to assume that the so-called 'humane' treatment of animals bred for their meat is being compromised. As with so many other things that are *big business*, money talks and, at the same time, often standards and principles can disappear. It wasn't that long ago here in the UK that we were all horrified to learn on the news how horse meat had found its way into almost every big brand name food supplier and supermarket. What can go wrong with a tin of chickpeas?

Consider the Planet

Okay, don't worry, I'm not going to start waving the *save the planet* banner here. However, it has to be said that our planet's current and projected meat consumption figures are not sustainable. We are chopping down the Amazon rainforest to clear sites to herd cattle. At the rate of the present rain forest destruction, it is estimated that the rain forests will be gone within just forty short years! This is a terrifying statistic.

When you consider that 20% of all the oxygen on earth comes from the Amazon rainforest, you can appreciate why the Amazon is often referred to as the *lungs of the earth*. Add to that, experts estimate that we are losing 137 plant, animal, and insect species every single day due to rainforest deforestation. That equates to 50,000 species a year. What's all that got to do with eating meat you might ask? Well, you might be shocked to learn that the leading cause of rainforest destruction is **animal agriculture**. In fact, animal agriculture is also the leading cause of global warming, not fossil fuels! If that last statement seems somewhat surprising, check out this link: **http://www.cowspiracy.com/facts/**

There is no question about it, eating a more plant-based diet has global benefits and certainly is a more compassionate, economical, and health promoting diet all round. It's a win, win, win situation!

Notice I use the term a 'plant-based diet' rather than vegetarian or vegan diet. Why is that? Well the terms *vegetarian* and *vegan* carry certain connotations and are often connected to various different causes and aims and therefore can have (to some people) negative connotations. Also, the terms vegan or vegetarian are labels and labels tend to put people in groups and putting people in groups can become divisive in my opinion, thus the 'us and them' mentality.

The term *plant-based diet* is far more *inclusive* and encompasses more people. It doesn't preclude eating animal products either. It might be argued that becoming vegetarian or vegan is not for everyone for lots of complex reasons, but almost *everyone* can include more plant-based foods in their diet and, as I mentioned, everyone wins if we do.

Okay, the rant is over and done with. You can now get onto the best part of the book—the food! Let's face it, that's the reason you bought this book in the first place, right? That leads me nicely to the final reason for *going veggie*—the **taste**! You will find that the recipes I have included in this book will not leave you feeling disappointed on the taste front and, as you make these dishes regularly, I'm convinced you'll never again view vegetable-based dishes as merely side orders, but rather as the main order.

Now, before we actually start cooking, we need to make sure we have everything we're going to need for these recipes, so I will discuss that in the next section of this book.

Spices We Will Be Using and Where You Might Find Them

Before we get cooking, we need to go shopping, so I'm going to send you on an errand to fetch some things you will need in order to make these dishes. I will also give you some tips on the best place to find these goodies.

Spices

These are the spices we will be using in these recipes. Some of these you may already have but some of them you might not. So, you cannot substitute one spice for another. If you want to achieve the right flavour you will need the right spices. Consider it an investment in your new cuisine. ☺

Black Mustard Seeds

These tiny, dark brown seeds are used in Indian cooking across many regions of India. They are particularly noted in Gujarati cuisine. They add an earthy pungency to a curry or dal, as well as decorate it—they look great peppered throughout the dish. You should be able to find these in any Asian/Indian wholesaler or store in your area. However, I will give you a few websites to have a look where you will almost certainly find what you need just in case you live in the Outer Hebrides and are lacking a good Asian store in your neighbourhood.

When buying black mustard seeds, it's worth buying them in 500 g bags or larger, as they keep well, and it's more economical to buy them that way. If the dish you are making calls for these in the recipe, then they will be the first whole spice in the pan when tempering, as they take longer than other spices to crackle and pop. In fact, watch out, as they often become little burning missiles if the pan is uncovered, and they can hurt if they land on you (believe me I know).

Fenugreek Seeds

These irregularly shaped seeds add pungency to any dish and, like the black mustard seeds, take a little while to crackle in the pan. So, if the dish you are making calls for them, put them in first or at the same time as the black mustard seeds. This spice has a distinct aroma often associated with curry and you may detect it coming through your pores the next day, but don't let that put you off using it. ☺

Cumin Seeds (Brown)

Where would we be without this whole spice? It features in almost all South Asian cooking and is the most used and most versatile of all the whole spices. When tempering these in the oil, be careful not to burn them, as they will make the curry taste awful if you do. Just fry them till they turn a light brown and give off their aroma.

Large Dried Red Chillies (Kashmiri Type)

These chillies are used for both flavour and to add colour to a dish. They are tempered in the oil with other whole spices. India is by far the greatest producer of these types of chillies and, there are many dishes incorporating them.

Cinnamon Stick

There can be quite a bit of confusion here because people can mistake cassia bark for cinnamon, as it looks similar and is sometimes referred to as cinnamon.

However, it is different, and we will be using actual cinnamon. Cinnamon sticks have many thin layers and grind easily in a coffee grinder, whereas cassia bark is very hard and doesn't grind easily. Cassia is milder and less intense than true cinnamon and cinnamon is also more expensive to buy—but worth it.

Asafoetida (a.k.a. Hing)

I call this 'Gujarati cuisines secret weapon.' Why? Because it is used extensively in Gujarati cooking, and it creates a flavour that is the *essence* of true Indian cooking. It also sets Gujarati cuisine apart from all other regional cuisines in India. This yellow crystal-like powder is used sparingly and is added during the tempering stage with other whole spices. When you cook with this 'Devil's dung' (as it is also known), it will fill your house with its pungent aroma. It's believed to cure flatulence, hence it is great with beans and pulses (if you know what I mean).

Green Cardamom

It is the world's third most expensive spice after saffron and vanilla. It is intensely aromatic with a resinous fragrance. You only need a little of this spice to add flavour to a dish and, in my opinion, it is best bought in its whole form in the husk, rather than just the seeds. Once those dark little seeds are removed from the husk, they quickly lose their flavour.

Curry Leaves

Curry leaves are those shiny, dark green, aromatic leaves of a tree from the citrus fruit family. They release a deliciously nutty aroma when fried in hot oil. Dried or fresh, they are a staple of South Indian cooking. Curry leaves are used in Indian and Southeast Asian cuisine in the same way bay leaves are used in the West. They really do smell like curry, hence the name.

Cloves

Cloves are the aromatic flower buds of a certain tree, and they are used in South Asian cuisine both in meat and vegetable dishes. Their carminative (prevention of gas) effect is said to increase hydrochloric acid in the stomach and thus aids peristalsis (contraction of the stomach and digestive tract). I'll bet you didn't know that. Neither did I till I Googled it. ☺

Methi Leaves

Methi leaves can transform a dish in my opinion. When I was seeking a way to replicate that takeaway curry taste, I discovered that methi leaves are a key flavour in BIR (British Indian Restaurant) cuisine.

Added in the hot oil or ghee at the tempering stage, they *ooze* flavour and pungency. In fact, I'm going to let you in on a little trade secret here; whenever we were quiet at Curry 2 Go (my takeaway business), I would take out a pan, add some oil, ginger, and garlic, get it on the stove, then in with the methi leaves. I would switch on the extractor fan and within *minutes* I would fill the streets of Chorley in and around our little takeaway with smells that would haul people in from the four corners of the earth. Honestly, this worked like magic! Methi leaves are not as pungent as their seed counterparts, but they are still quite potent.

Panch Phoran

Panch phoran literally means *five spices*. This whole spice blend usually includes fenugreek, black mustard, nigella, cumin, and fennel in equal parts. It can be spelt different ways, e.g.

pach phoron, panch puran, and even padkaune masala. Unlike other spice blends, it is only ever used whole, never ground.

Kokum

Garcinia indica is a plant in the mangosteen family. The outer layer of the fruit is dried to create an ingredient used as a souring agent. It is often used in place of tamarind.

Powdered Spices You Will Need

Deggi Mirch (Deep Red Chilli Powder)

This dark red chilli powder is made from high quality dark red chillies or a mixture of different varieties known for their flavour more than their heat. Often, the commercial varieties of chilli powder that we get from the supermarkets are not very flavourful, but they are hotter than the deggi mirch brand you can buy at the store. Often that is because they grind the seeds with the chillies, hence that chilli powder is often an orange colour rather than the deep read of the deggi mirch brand. If you cannot get deggie mirch where you are, here is a great tip to make your own. Take your regular hot chilli powder and mix it 50/50 with a good quality paprika, and you will have something that resembles the deggi mirch product.

Turmeric

Do you know the yellow stuff that stains your best white shirt and just won't come out? Yes, it's turmeric. Turmeric doesn't add a particularly distinct flavour, but it adds that bitter element that is essential to a good curry. It also adds a woody note to a dish, not to mention colour. It needs to be used sparingly, as too much can make a dish too bitter.

Coriander

This is one spice that I grind fresh myself along with cumin because the difference between this and the shop-bought variety is like night and day. I've noticed that the best Indian and Pakistani restaurants (where I have had the privilege of getting behind the kitchen doors) grind their own coriander and cumin.

Freshly ground coriander has a distinctive fruity aroma and taste, and that is missing with the shop-bought commercial varieties. If you don't have a spice grinder, get one or get a pestle and mortar. The liberal use of coriander in certain dishes gives that aromatic quality to the dish.

Cumin

Basically, everything I have just said above applies to cumin, except that cumin is a tad more potent in imbuing a spicier element to a dish than coriander is. In fact, curry would not taste like curry *without* cumin. Did you know that toasted cumin can be used as a finishing spice to a dish much like garam masala is used? Try adding it to a hot and spicy dish like Madras.

***

Okay, essentially, those are the spices we will be utilising in the Quick & Easy Vegetarian Curry Recipes in this book. Hopefully, if you are already a curry aficionado, you may already have all these spices. If you are fairly new to this curry cooking thing, then you may be lamenting the fact that you don't have most of these ingredients and perhaps you're not sure where to get them.

Let me help you out. Firstly, you may be surprised to learn that the nearest big supermarket actually stocks most of these spices; however, this is generally not the smart way to buy them. You will pay top dollar for a small 100 g jar or packet, where you could get a 500 g pack for about the same price from an Asian store.

If you are not familiar with where the nearest Asian stores are, ask yourself 'Where is the nearest Asian community? Where is the nearest Mosque or Hindu temple?' Undoubtedly, if you can locate these, you will find nearby spice shops, halal butchers, etc.

If you know for certain that the nearest Asian community is an aeroplane ride away, then you may need to look at online websites that sell everything you need and more. In the UK, there are lots of these and many are very reasonably priced, so you can order from the comfort of your sofa and have them shipped to your home in a few days. Also, some of the ones I list below actually deliver outside the UK to Europe and beyond. ☺

Spice Blends (Masalas)

Chaat Masala

This masala (mixture) is usually a blend of cumin, coriander, amchoor (dried mango powder), ginger powder, and hing. This is a potent spice mixture used to add sharpness to a dish. Used in a similar way to garam masala, this spice blend will lift the simplest of dishes and add a salty sour flavour. You will usually find this in the boxed spice blends in a good Asian supermarket.

Garam Masala

Garam masala is a seven-spice blend that can vary from region to region in India. For example, the Gujarati versions of garam masala tend to have upwards of thirteen spices in them and they add an incredible pungency to Gujarati style dishes. Garam masala is generally used as a finishing spice. In other words, it is added at the end of the cooking process or just before serving the dish. When used in small quantities, garam masala has the ability to lift all the other spices in the dish and take a curry or dal to another level.

The commercial varieties of garam masala are very different from the home-made varieties. For example, in India, rather than roast the spices prior to grinding them, they dry them out in the sun. This is a much more gentle process that creates a garam masala that is much more flavourful. Why not try making your own? You can find a recipe for garam masala on my YouTube channel. Simply type my name, Julian Voigt, into YouTube and you will find my channel, then you type in *garam masala* in the search bar.

Tandoori Masala

I usually describe this masala (mixture) as garam masala on steroids. I think that is a good description because, basically, tandoori masala has all the typical seven spices found in garam masala but added to those are dried garlic, ginger, cayenne pepper, fenugreek, cardamom, mustard seeds, and red food colouring. We will be using this spice blend in a delicious vegetable tikka masala dish.

***

So, if you don't already have them, make sure you buy these spices before cooking any of these dishes. There is nothing worse than being in a creative mood to cook a curry only to find part way into the process that you are missing one or more spices. ☹

Now, if you have looked through the list of spices and spotted one or more spices that you don't have, or are not sure where to get them from, the next section of this book should help you.

Online Stores That Sell Spices and South Asian Foodstuffs

http://www.theasiancookshop.co.uk/

This online store delivers to most of the UK and the islands as well as most European destinations. They have a reasonably good selection and prices are reasonable. They also have a blog with various recipes.

http://www.thespiceshop.co.uk/shop

This online store caters for West Indian and Afro Caribbean cuisine as well as South Asian. The selection is limited and prices are more expensive than some of the others.

https://www.spicesofindia.co.uk/

This is probably the best-known source for online sales of South Asian spices. This website has an excellent and varied selection, and they stock all the well-known and utilised brands like Patak's and Rajah. Prices are very reasonable and certain lines are quite cheap. You can also buy kitchen utensils from this website that are used in Asian households. They ship all over the UK and Channel Islands and to almost anywhere in Europe. Delivery in the UK is free.

http://spicemountain.co.uk/

This website has a varied selection of spices, even some obscure difficult-to-find spices. However, they do not stock the well-known brands like some of the other websites do. Prices are reasonable, and they do ship to most European countries.

* * *

Julian Voigt

Now that you know where to get the spices we will be using, go and get them! You will also note on most of these sites that you can buy all the various dals, beans and pulses, so make sure you get those too. And that leads nicely into our next subject—dals!

The 'Oh So Hallowed Dal'

"Dal is to India what rice is to China."—Me, I said that. ☺

Dhal or dal (you may see it spelt either way), simply refers to a dried pulse, lentil, pea, or bean—all of which come under the umbrella of dal. If the dish being made is wet, it's referred to as a dal. If the dish being made with lentils, beans, or any pulse is dry, it's called a kathoor in Gujarati.

As already mentioned in this book, most of India is vegetarian and dals provide them with an excellent protein source. Most dals are typically around 25% protein.

I'm going to get on my soap box again here, highlighting the excellent nutritional value of dals, so stick with it! Hopefully, after reading this section, your appreciation for dals will increase and you'll be eager to get cooking with them.

Have you ever wandered up and down the aisle of the dals section of an Indian grocers or cash and carry and just been amazed at the sheer variety of different pulses, beans, legumes, and lentils? Did you muse to yourself, "What do they do with all these pulses?" It was the same curiosity that caused me to explore the wonderful world of dals, as well as my decision a few years back to adopt a vegetarian diet.

I'm so glad I did, as it opened up to me a world of foods that I had previously not discovered. When some people think of adopting a more plant-based diet, they may approach it negatively thinking that, because the diet doesn't include meat, it is thought of in terms of deficiency or deprivation. They focus on what is missing, whereas I have come to view it in the reverse. I see a diet of far greater variety and superior nutrition.

I often think that I might not have discovered these rich and interesting foods had I left the meat on my plate (if you get where I'm coming from).

Don't get me wrong, I'm not saying you have to become a vegetarian to explore the variety that comes from plant-based foods. I'm just saying that we can limit our diet when the meal revolves around animal protein. Nobody would disagree that including more plant-based foods in our diet is a good thing. I would add that it makes your food more enjoyable and enriching to boot!

The Good Stuff and None of the Bad

The great thing about beans, pulses, peas, and lentils is that they are high in protein, and they are also an excellent source of fibre. Many people choose to eat meat for its protein, but meat contains no fibre—that's right—none.

Fibre is an essential element in keeping our digestive tract and bowels healthy. India has one of the *lowest* rates of bowel cancer in the world and this has been credited to their lifelong vegetarian diet. Even those who do eat meat in India eat much smaller quantities than most of us here in the West. They consume *way* more plant-based foods than they do animal-based foods, and they eat very little processed foods.

A Westernised Pakistani friend of mine, who was born and raised here in the UK, refers to dals as a 'poor man's curry.' That is because in India the majority of the population are poor and to them dal is an inexpensive meal. However, from what I have seen, most Indians who are poor *choose* to eat dals, not because they can't afford anything else but because they love them!

Dals are tasty, satisfying, and incredibly varied and versatile. I *love* dals and could eat them every night of the week.

In East India and Nepal, the term 'dal bhat' means dal with rice. When you think about it, it's a perfectly balanced meal. You have a good source of protein and fibre in the dhal combined with a carbohydrate in the rice. No wonder many, yes, *'poor'* people in India live to be a hundred and stay active—many of them still work well into their eighties.

On the other hand, we in the West are suffering from the many so called 'diseases of affluence.' We need to take a few lessons from those *'poor'* dal-loving Indians and develop a love for them ourselves. What do you think?

Nutritional Facts about Dals

Beans, which are included in many dal recipes like mung, kidney, and chori, are packed full of essential minerals which many of us could be missing from our diet—like magnesium, potassium, selenium, and zinc. Also, beans, legumes, and pulses contain a compound called phytates (also known as phytic acid). Recent studies have shown that this compound has powerful anti-cancer properties—another reason perhaps why those 'poor' dal-loving Indians have such low rates of bowel and other cancers?

Lower Cholesterol

Beans and lentils help lower blood cholesterol as they contain high levels of soluble fibre. Lowering cholesterol levels has been proven to reduce the risk of heart disease and diabetes. In fact, scientists in Canada ran tests on patients who suffered from PAD (peripheral artery disease) and found that when those patients ate four to six portions of lentils, beans, or legumes, their arteries showed signs of a reversal of the disease.

Heart Health

Lentils and beans contain folate (folic acid) and magnesium (a mineral that many of us here in the West are deficient in). Both folic acid and magnesium are great contributors to heart health. For example, folate lowers the homocysteine levels in the blood (a serious risk for heart disease). Woman planning to have babies have been told about the importance of folic acid in the healthy development of their babies. So, that's another good reason to eat dals.

Stabilise Blood Sugar

Diabetes is on the rise in the West and this is largely due to the Western diet. A diet rich in fruits and vegetables (including legumes) helps to stabilise blood sugar. In other words, it stops the insulin spikes. Beans, lentils, and pulses are low on the glycaemic index, thus they help to stabilise blood sugar.

Weight Loss

I know you're probably thinking, "How can eating more dals help me to lose weight?" It works this way. Fibre and protein rich foods (like dals) keep us feeling fuller longer, hence when we include ample amounts of these in our diet, then the net effect is that we eat less of *other stuff* (like fatty foods and refined carbohydrates). We will also tend to snack less between meals. And, the overall net result? We consume fewer calories and, if we are overweight, we will see those unwanted pounds coming off. ☺

Satisfaction Guaranteed!

Don't worry, I'm not going to break out in song here but, when it comes to the wonderful world of dals, satisfaction is guaranteed! What do I mean? Well the great thing about dals is that there are so *many* of them. The next time you're wandering the isles of your favourite South Asian grocers, take a wander down the dried lentils/bean/pea isle, and there you'll see a plethora of different dried peas, beans, and legumes—many of which you will never have laid eyes on before. They have different tastes, textures, and colours. There is no shortage of variety here and there are no shortage of dal recipes to be enjoyed either. As the sub heading to this paragraph suggests, those recipes are very tasty and satisfying too.

The one thing I have noticed about eating dals on a regular basis is just how satisfying a meal they make. For example, if I occasionally (it is occasional, honest!) eat something I know I shouldn't (like something deep fried), I always regret it about twenty minutes after eating it. I feel the indigestion coming on not to mention the lethargy. My body lets me know in no uncertain terms that it's not happy with the food choice I just made, whereas, when I eat dal, it's quite the reverse.

When I eat dal I never suffer indigestion or bloating, and it doesn't slow me down either. I almost feel my belly smiling as if to say, 'You got it right this time.' Also, because these are fibre rich foods, there are no roadblocks the following day (if you get what I mean!).

Here, for your interest, is a list of various dals and dal recipes, many of which I will feature in this book.

Mung Dal (Mung Beans Split)

This is one of my favourites. These split small dark green beans have an almost creamy texture when cooked. They make an incredible gravy when you crush a few of them after they are cooked into the sauce. They also have a fantastic taste. We will be making a split mung dal with spinach, kindly contributed by Dan and Priti of the Chapatti Café in Chorlton, Manchester.

Toor Dal

Toor dal, as it is known in Hindi, is also known as pigeon pea. This dal provides a high level of protein and the important amino acids methionine, tryptophan, and lysine. An interesting fact about tryptophan is that it is a natural antidepressant and mood elevator, hence another reason why dals are very satisfying. This dal makes a delicious yellow-coloured soup that is used in Gujarati dal—lightly spiced and served with whole-wheat chapattis. Yum, it's making me hungry just thinking about it.

Channa Dal

Basically, channa dal is small dried split chickpeas. They make a tasty dal and have a unique slightly sweet flavour. These little split dried chickpeas take a little longer to cook compared with other dals, but they're worth it! They add a delicious texture to a dish and are great mixed with other dals, as in the case of Punjabi Dal Fry, which is featured in this book.

Mung Beans

Mung beans are my favourite of all the dals because they are *so* tasty and versatile. They are protein packed and are very satisfying. Mung beans are incredibly versatile and are used to make a variety of foods from dals to pancakes. They are even used to make a type of pasta thanks to their high starch content. We will be featuring this bean in my Mung Bean Curried Stew recipe.

Masoor Dal

These are the red lentils readily available everywhere. These lentils are predominantly the ones that Indian restaurants use for tarka dal. The reason is that they cook quickly, and they are inexpensive. We will be using them in some recipes in this book.

Rajma

Rajma is simply kidney beans. The kidney bean is not indigenous to India but was brought there by the Portuguese. They quickly became popular in northern Indian cuisine and rajma dal has become a very popular Punjabi dish. It is both pungent and spicy and usually made with a thick gravy. The recipe is this book is quick and easy to make and very tasty.

Urad Dal

Black dal (urad) is used mixed with other lentils for a fantastic texture and flavour. Also, these small beans are ground to a powder and are used to make poppadoms (bet you didn't know that!). They are also used to make the batter for the dosa—a kind of pancake filled with a sweet and savoury filling.

* * *

The reason I included this section dedicated to dals is because we will feature many recipes that are made with dals. In fact, it would be correct to say that any vegetarian Indian cook book that didn't feature dals would be very much out of touch with what people in India actually eat (vegetarian or non-vegetarian). Dals are to India what rice is to china. ☺

Cooking Time

I will provide a guide here for the cooking times for various dals. However, as this cookbook is all about quick and easy cooking, I'm going to *urge* you to buy a pressure cooker if you don't already have one. I can honestly tell you that no Indian household would be complete without a pressure cooker. In fact, the pressure cooker is never off the hob in an Asian house.

If you do a search on YouTube for a dal recipe, you will see that all the cooks use a pressure cooker. *They are a must!* When it comes to timings when using a pressure cooker, the time will vary from pressure cooker to pressure cooker depending on its size, the volume of food inside the pressure cooker, and the temperature you are cooking with. You will notice that many Indian cooks use the term 'whistle blasts' as the measuring gauge. This simply refers to the time it takes the pressure cooker to reach pressure then release some of that pressure with a 'whistle blast' (which simply means that the whistle or valve on top of the pressure cooker rises and let's off a blast).

Here's a guide to cooking dals with and without a pressure cooker. Keep in mind, however, that you will not be cooking many of these recipes in the twenty minutes or less that the book promises if you don't use a pressure cooker; so get one!

	Pressure Cooker Times	Conventional Boiling Times
Mung beans whole	8 minutes	60-70 minutes
Mung beans split with skin	6 minutes	25-30 minutes
Urad dal	10 minutes	60-70 minutes
Chickpeas while brown	20 minutes	70-90 minutes
Channa (split chickpeas)	15 minutes	60-70 minutes
Masoor dal (red lentils)	5 minutes	30 minutes
Toor (pigeon pea whole)	15-20 minutes	70-90 minutes
Tuver (pigeon pea split)	7-9 minutes	30-40 minutes
Rajma (kidney beans)	15 minutes	70-90 minutes

One final thing: all dals require that you wash them thoroughly and, preferably, soak them before use. You will want to wash them in a bowl till the water is clear and soak them for at least one hour before use. Most Asian households soak them the night before.

Hopefully, you are now inspired and eager to start cooking. So, what we are waiting for!

Recipes—Let's Get Cooking!

For our first recipe, we're going to start with a taste of Gujarat. This very tasty dal is often served quite runny, more like a soup than a curry. However, you can decide whether to have it a little thicker or runny, as it is traditionally served. The recipe will explain how.

Gujarati Dal

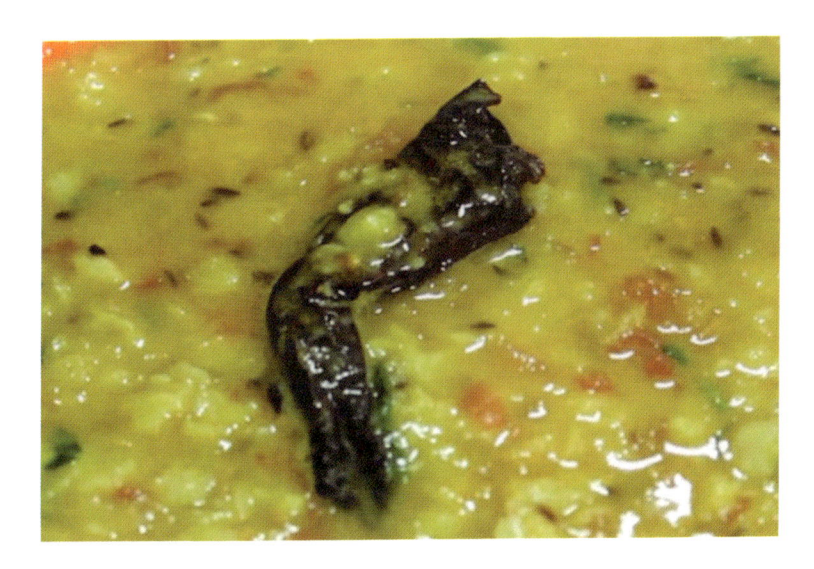

This recipe utilises toor dal and is also known as pigeon pea. The recipe will start first with ingredients then follow with cooking method, followed by a 'Chef's tip'— that extra something to help you get the best from this recipe.

Serves 4. Prep & Cook time about 15 minutes.

Ingredients:

1 cup of washed toor dal

2 large dried red chillies

2-3 TBSP of vegetable oil

1 TBSP of butter ghee

1 tsp of black mustard seeds

1 h/tsp of brown cumin seeds

2 cloves

1/2 tsp of hing (asafoetida)

1 TBSP of curry leaves

2 stick pieces of cinnamon

2 kokum (if you can't source this you can use tamarind instead)

Salt to taste

1 tomato chopped

Jaggery goor 1" piece

Method:

Add the washed toor dal to your pressure cooker and add two times the same volume of water as the lentils. Bring to pressure and wait till you hear 3 whistles (about 5 minutes) then remove from the heat. To cool the pan down quickly, place the pan under cold running water for a minute. Now, release the pressure carefully by removing the whistle (CAUTION! Hot steam can burn you! Use an oven glove).

Once the pan has lost all of its pressure, carefully remove the lid and set the cooked toor dal aside.

Tempering

Next, we will temper the whole spices. Heat the oil in the pan. Once it's hot, add in the black mustard seeds. As they start to pop and crackle, add the cumin seeds, dried red chillies, cloves, hing, and the dried curry leaves and stir. Be careful not to burn the spices, so make sure the oil is not smoking. If it does smoke, simply remove the pan from the heat. Next, add in the tomato. This will cool things down.

Now, add in the cooked toor dal and mix well with the spices. Add in some water—you decide now how runny or thick you like it, but I would suggest that you add a bit more water than you think, as we can reduce this later.

Add in the powdered spices, then the salt, jaggery, and kokum. Mix all the ingredients well and simmer vigorously for about 8 minutes, then reduce the heat and simmer for a further 2 minutes.

The Gujarati dal is almost done, check for seasoning and adjust according to taste. Add in the butter ghee; this will add a delicious silky texture to your dal, not to mention flavour too! Serve with delicious hot chapattis and some plain boiled rice. Yummy!

> Chef's Tip: Add both the coriander and ghee literally just before serving. You will get more punch from the coriander and flavor from the ghee. ☺

Bengali Egg Curry

This next recipe is a taste of Bengal. This delicious egg curry will satisfy all those who like dishes that are spicy and full of pungent flavours. If you have not yet had an egg curry, then you don't know what you're missing, because eggs and curry go so well together. *Trust me; you've got to try it!*

Serves 3. Prep & Cook time 20 minutes.

Ingredients:

6 hard-boiled eggs (I recommend organic free-range eggs. They just taste better.)
3 TBSP of oil
1 TBSP of crushed garlic
2 dried red chillies
2 tins of crushed tomatoes
3 large onions

1 tsp of turmeric powder

1 TBSP of deggi mirch (red chilli powder)

4 green chillies chopped (Asian variety)

1 TBSP of mustard seed powder

1/2 tsp of garam masala

1 TBSP of coriander powder

1 tsp of cumin powder

A handful of fresh coriander including the stalks

1 tsp of salt

1 tsp of brown sugar

1 cup of boiling water

Method:

First, take your 3 onions and peel them. Blend these into a paste and then set aside for later. Next, hard-boil the 6 eggs. When they're done, set them aside in cold water. This will make them easier to peel later.

Next, take a large frying pan or other wide-bottomed pan, add in the oil, and turn on the heat. Once the oil is hot, add in the dried red chillies. After a minute, add in the crushed garlic and fry this till it just starts to turn golden brown. Now, in with the onions, sugar, and green chillies. Fry this mixture until the onion starts turning brown (it's important for the right flavour!).

Now, add in all the powdered spices except for the garam masala and fry the spices for 1–2 minutes, after which add in the tomatoes. Add in about a cup full of boiling water to thin the sauce and return it to a vigorous simmer.

Next, we take the boiled eggs that have been sitting in the cold water and peel them and give them a quick rinse to ensure that all the shell is removed (nothing worse than chowing down on a bit of eggshell☹). Once cleaned, take the eggs and prick them with a fork. This accomplishes two things: 1) it stops the eggs from falling apart in the curry, and 2) it helps the eggs to draw in those flavours in the sauce.

Now, add the eggs to the sauce and cook together for another 8 minutes. You will know the curry is ready as the oil should start to float to the top (doesn't that look great!). Finish the dish by adding in the coriander and the garam masala. Done!

> Chef's Tip: Don't serve this dish piping hot, as you won't appreciate all the subtle flavours. Let it stand for about 3-4 minutes before serving. Enjoy!

Cauliflower & Pea Curry

This curry is made with a delicious yoghurt gravy—and I mean *delicious!* In India, cauliflower is eaten in many dishes, which reminds me of a comment made by celebrity TV Chef Rick Stein who said, 'In India, cauliflower is the poor man's meat . . . .'

Whether or not it's the poor man's meat, I don't know, but I do know that cauliflower has the ability to absorb the flavours of things it's cooked with and this dish is no exception.

Serves 2-3. Prep and cook time about 20 minutes.

Ingredients:

3 cups of cauliflower florets
1 cup of peas (fresh or frozen)
1/2 cup of plain low-fat yoghurt
2 TBSP of chopped coriander

1/2 tsp of garam masala

1 to 1-1/2 cups of water

2 TBSP of oil

1/2 tsp of cumin seeds

2 dried red chillies

1/4 tsp of hing

2 TBSP of besan (chickpea flour)

1 TBSP of garlic & ginger paste

1 tsp of deggi mirch (chilli powder)

1/2 tsp of turmeric powder

1 h/tsp of coriander powder (freshly ground)

1 tsp of jaggery goor (brown sugar will do)

Salt to taste

Method:

Heat the oil over a moderate heat and, once the oil is hot, add in the cumin seeds. When they start to crackle, add in the garlic & ginger paste and cook that for about a minute.

Next, add in the dried red chillies and the hing.

Now, add in the besan and stir till it forms a paste. Keep stirring so that the mixture doesn't stick to the bottom of the pan.

Add in the yoghurt. Turn down the heat and keep stirring to ensure that the yoghurt doesn't separate in the pan.

After about one minute, add the turmeric, deggi mirch, coriander powder, salt, and jaggery. Once they're mixed in, add the peas. Cook this mixture together, while continuing to stir, to keep the yoghurt from separating.

Next, add in the cauliflower and a little boiling water to get the gravy to the right consistency. Lower the heat to a medium to high simmer, cover, and let it cook a further 10-15 minutes or until the cauliflower is cooked or just turning tender.

Once done, add in the fresh coriander and garam masala. Allow to stand off the heat for a minute and then serve. This curry is delicious with a naan bread or rice.

> Chef's Tip: Serve in a bowl with plenty of sauce and hot naan bread drizzled with butter ghee, and it doesn't get much better than that!

Dal Toori

I got this recipe from the head chef at the Zaffran Indian restaurant in Old Town Puerto Del Carmen Lanzarote. I made a video of the chef cooking this recipe, but the quality of the video was poor, as I shot it on my wife's mobile phone. Despite that, I got a flurry of positive comments underneath the video saying how tasty it was. Hence, I decided to feature it in this book. If you want to see the video, go to my YouTube channel (Julian Voigt) and type 'Zaffran Lanzarote' in the search bar.

Serves 2. Prep & Cook about time 20 minutes.

Ingredients:

2 TBSP of butter ghee

1/2 tsp of cumin seeds

1 medium red onion finely chopped

1 TBSP of garlic & ginger paste

1 tsp of methi leaves

1 tsp of garam masala

1/2 tsp of turmeric powder

1/2 tsp of deggi mirch

2 tomatoes chopped

1 TBSP of tomato puree

2 medium sized courgettes (zucchini) cut into thick slices with the skin

1 cup of pre-cooked toor dal

A handful of fresh coriander

1 cup of water

Salt to taste

1 TBSP of lemon Juice.

Method:

First, you will need to pre-cook the courgette (zucchini) in a little oil in a frying pan just until it starts to turn golden brown (for a healthier version, see Chef's Tip below).

Heat the butter ghee in the pan and, once it's hot, add in the cumin seeds; they should crackle indicating the oil is hot enough.

After about 30 seconds, add in the methi leaves, garlic & ginger paste, and fry together for about 1 minute.

Add the onion and cook it till it begins to turn translucent.

Now, add in the fresh tomato, deggi mirch, turmeric, and salt. After you have fried the powdered spices for a minute or so, add the water (make sure it's hot so you don't bring the temperature of the pan down).

Now, add in the tomato puree. Mix everything together in the pan, add in the cooked courgette and the pre-cooked toor dal, and bring it all to a vigorous simmer. Cook the mixture for about 4-5 minutes, then turn down the heat and add in the fresh coriander, garam masala, and lemon juice. One quick stir and it's ready to serve. *Delicious!*

> Chef's Tip: For a healthier version (as well as adding a slightly charred taste), cook the courgettes on a griddle till they turn light golden brown.

Khadi (Hot Yoghurt Soup)

Khadi is popular all over India and there are many variations of this dish, but the one I like is the Gujarati khadi which has that slightly sweet taste that works so well with the yoghurt gravy. Interestingly, the dish was served to Barack Obama on one of his recent trips to India, and he loved it! This dish usually forms part of a tarli—a compartmentalised tray with a selection of vegetarian dishes on it. Khadi works well served up with a sumptuous vegetable curry and a couple of chapattis. For a vegan version of this dish, replace the ghee with vegetable oil and replace the yoghurt with a soya alternative or a coconut yoghurt, which you can buy from most big supermarkets.

Serves 2-3. Prep & cook time about 20 minutes.

Ingredients:
2 TBSP of oil
1 cup of yoghurt

3 cups of water
3–4 TBSP of besan (chick pea flour)
1/2 tsp of turmeric powder
1/2 tsp of ginger powder
Salt to taste
1 tsp of butter ghee
1 whole dried red chilli
3 clove
1/2 tsp of fenugreek seeds
1 piece of cinnamon
1/3 tsp of hing
1/2 tsp of cumin seeds
1/2 tsp of black mustard seeds
A handful of fresh coriander leaves
1 TBSP of curry leaves

Method:

Take a bowl, add the yoghurt, besan, water, turmeric, and ginger powder and mix well, preferably with a blender. Add to a pan and heat gently, making sure to *keep stirring* the mixture to prevent it from forming clumps.

Tempering

Next, we're going to temper our spices. Add the oil and butter ghee to a pre-heated frying pan. Once they're hot, add in the black mustard seeds and, as soon as they begin to pop (watch out—they're like little burning missiles!), add in the cumin seeds, fenugreek seeds, and the curry leaves.

Next, in with the red chilli and hing. By now, the oil and ghee will be very hot, so remove the pan from the heat and stir. Now, take the tempered spices, oil, and ghee and add them to the Khadi, which should be simmering away nicely. *Again, make sure you keep stirring this mixture* or it will separate. Next, add in the fresh coriander, jaggery, and salt. Simmer for 3 or 4 more minutes, and it's done!

> Chef's Tip: This dish is best served with a variety of other dishes, say as part of a thali. It goes great as an accompaniment with spicier dishes like Punjabi Dal Fry (on the next page).☺

Punjabi Dal Fry

This recipe will incorporate three types of dal: split mung dal, red lentil (masoor dal), and toor dal. Before making this dish, don't forget to wash the dals and soak them for at least one hour before cooking or overnight. This flavoursome dal has quite a dry consistency, which lends to its stronger flavour.

Serves 4-5. Prep & cook time about 20 minutes.

Ingredients:

1/2 cup masoor dal (red lentils)
1/2 cup toor dal (pigeon pea)
1/2 cup mung dal (split mung beans with skin)
4 TBSP of butter ghee
1 tsp of black mustard seeds
1 tsp of cumin seeds

2 dried red chillies (Kashmiri type)

1/3 tsp of hing

3 green chillies chopped (Asian variety)

1 red onion sliced

1 tsp of crushed garlic

1 tsp of chopped root ginger

2 tomatoes chopped

1 tsp of deggi mirch (good quality chilli powder—NOT extra hot)

1 tsp of garam masala

1 tsp of turmeric

1 tsp of coriander powder

1 tsp of cumin powder

1 TBSP of lemon juice

Salt to taste

Method:

Put the 3 dals into a pressure cooker for 3 whistles—which is about 10–12 minutes from when the pressure cooker has reached full pressure. Once the dals are cooked, set the cooked dals aside for use later. They should be soft but not mushy. If you are cooking the dals without a pressure cooker, refer to the section 'All about Dals' for cooking times.

Now to prepare the spice mixture or *tarka* as it is referred to. Heat the pan on a medium to high heat and add the butter ghee. Once the ghee is hot, add in the black mustard seeds first. When they start to pop, add the cumin seeds, dried red chillies, and the hing.

After these spices have fried for about one minute, add the onion, green chillies, garlic, and chopped ginger and cook these for another 3–4 minutes, or until the onions start to turn translucent.

Next, add in the chopped tomatoes and mix these with the spices. After these have cooked for 2–3 minutes, it's time to add in the powdered spices.

Add in the deggi mirch, garam masala, coriander, cumin, and turmeric. Stir well and cook the spices for about 1 minute. If the mixture in the pan is too dry, add a little boiling water—this will allow you to push the spices a little further and extract more flavour from them.

Next, add in the cooked dals and some boiling water to achieve the correct consistency. If you add too much, don't panic, as you can simply reduce it by cooking it for a little longer.

Next, add in the salt and cook for a further 5 minutes with the pan covered.

After 5 minutes, stir the mixture, add the fresh lemon juice, and adjust the seasoning to taste.

Finally, garnish with some fresh coriander.

> Chef's Tip: With spicier dishes like this one, it always works well to add some of the coriander stalks finely chopped up. You can also try substituting lemon with lime.

Cabbage Curry (VV)

I bet I can guess what you're thinking as you come across this recipe. Well, let me tell you that this is one of the *tastiest* vegetable dishes I have ever had! There is something about the combination of spices and cabbage that work *so* well. I can't look at a cabbage in a supermarket these days without thinking of cabbage curry. This dish is so tasty that you can eat it on its own or with a chapatti and some pickles—*it's amazing!*

Serves 2-3. Prep & Cook time 20 minutes.

Ingredients:

3/4 of a medium white cabbage
3 TBSP of vegetable oil
1 tsp of black mustard seeds
1/3 tsp of hing
1 tsp of cumin seeds

A pinch of panch phoran

1 medium sliced onion

1 stick of cinnamon

1 TBSP of crushed garlic

1 tsp of chopped ginger

A few dried curry leaves

1 tsp of dried methi leaves

3 green chillies chopped

1 tsp of each of: deggi mirch, cumin powder, coriander powder, and turmeric

1 tsp of brown sugar

1 large tomato chopped

Half a green pepper thinly sliced

A handful of fresh coriander

1/2 a tsp of salt

2 cups of water

Method:

Heat the oil in the pan and, when it's hot, add the black mustard seeds. Once they start to pop, add the panch phoran, cumin seeds, methi leaves, curry leaves, cinnamon, and the hing. Fry these in the oil for about 1 minute, so they can release their flavours into the oil.

Next, add in the onion, chillies, garlic, ginger, and sugar. Mix well and put the lid on the pan. Allow these ingredients to cook together for another 6–8 minutes, or until the onions have turned slightly brown.

Next, take off the lid and add the powdered spices: the deggi mirch, cumin, coriander, and turmeric. Cook these spices for a further 2–3 minutes, ensuring that all the spices are cooked. Add the salt. If the mixture becomes too dry, add a little boiling water to help push your spices further and get the most out of them.

Next, add in the chopped tomato, stir, and cook for about 1–2 minutes.

Add in the sliced green pepper, cabbage, and the 2 cups of water (make sure the water is boiling or you will slow down the cooking process). Mix well.

Return the lid to the pan and cook for a further 8–10 minutes, or until the cabbage is soft.

When the cabbage is soft, add in the fresh coriander and stir once. Leave the curry to stand for 2–3 minutes, then serve. Done!

> Chef's Tip: This curry is delicious served with a nice soft wholemeal chapatti and some chilli pickle and/or mango chutney, or try serving this as part of a thali.

Rajma (VV)

When we think of kidney beans, we generally think of chilli con carne. This Punjabi dish takes the humble kidney bean and turns it into something special. In many Indian homes, rajma is often thought of as a special dish. This sumptuous dish is tasty and the spice combinations in this recipe work really well with kidney beans. After eating this dish, you may not look at the humble kidney bean the same way again. For convenience, and in keeping with the *quick* theme of this book, we are using tinned kidney beans, but feel free to cook your own as per the cooking guidelines in the 'All about Dals' section.

Serves 2. Prep & Cook time about 15 minutes.

Ingredients:

4 TBSP of vegetable oil
1 tin of kidney beans drained and rinsed

1 large onion

2 large tomatoes (the riper the better)

6–8 garlic cloves chopped fine

1 inch piece of fresh root ginger chopped

1 tsp of cumin seeds

1 tsp of turmeric powder

1 tsp of deggi mirch (or good quality dark red chilli powder)

1 TBSP of coriander powder (preferably freshly ground for this dish)

1 tsp of cumin powder

1 tsp of garam masala

1/2 tsp of salt

2 cups of water

Method:

Heat the pan, add in the oil and, once it's hot, add in the cumin seeds. They should crackle. After about 1 minute, add in the garlic and ginger and fry until the garlic turns a light brown.

Next, add in the onion and fry this until it turns translucent.

Now add in these powdered spices: cumin, turmeric, coriander, and chilli powder. Fry these for about 1–2 minutes. Again, if the mixture becomes too dry, add in a little boiling water to loosen the mixture.

Once the spices are cooked, add in the chopped tomatoes and the salt, stir well, and cook with the lid on the pan for about 4–5 minutes.

Now, add in the kidney beans and mix well. Add the 2 cups of water (make sure it's boiling so it won't slow down the cooking process). Mix well and simmer on a medium to high heat for another 6–7 minutes. Make sure the mixture is *thick,* not runny, before serving. Add in the garam masala and stir into the mixture. Taste and adjust seasoning. Allow the curry to stand for 2 minutes before serving. It's nice with plain boiled rice. *Delicious!*

> Chef's Tip: When stirring this curry in the pan, make sure to use a wooden spoon and stir gently so you don't break all the kidney beans.

Aubergine & Peanut Curry (VV)

This is one of my all-time favourites and one my wife loves. The addition of peanuts in this curry makes this one not only *super tasty* but also very satisfying. Peanuts are protein packed and help keep hunger at bay. So, if you're looking for a veggie curry to satisfy on all fronts, then this could be the one for you.

Serves 2-3. Prep & Cook time 20 minutes.

Ingredients:

100 g of whole unsalted peanuts

1 large aubergine (eggplant) cut into chunks

3 medium ripe tomatoes roughly chopped

2–3 green chillies (Asian variety) chopped

3 cloves of garlic crushed

1 inch piece of fresh root ginger finely chopped

1 large onion roughly chopped
3–4 TBSP of vegetable oil
1 tsp of brown cumin
1/2 tsp of turmeric powder
1 tsp of brown sugar
Salt to taste
1/2 tsp of garam masala
1/2 to 1 cup of water
1 TBSP of fresh coriander

Method:

First, take the aubergine and cut it into nice big chunks. I slice it in half lengthways, and then repeat the same with the two halves, and then cut across the aubergine, so that what you have are two-inch pieces. If you cut them too small, they will go to mush and almost disappear in the pan.

Once you have cut the aubergine, shallow fry it in a little vegetable oil just enough until it begins to turn a golden brown. Once it has, remove it from the pan, place it on some kitchen paper to remove the excess oil, and set it aside.

Next, take the same pan used to fry the aubergine (hopefully there is still a little oil left in the pan), return the pan to a medium heat and, when the oil is hot, add in the peanuts and roast them gently *making sure to keep them moving in the pan so they don't burn!*

After 2–3 minutes, they should start to change colour to a golden brown and perhaps begin to break up. Once this happens, remove them from the pan and give them a quick pounding in a pestle and mortar, just enough to break them up—we don't want them whole in this curry but we don't want them crushed to a powder either. Once that is done, set them aside.

Next, add the oil in the pan and heat. Once the oil is hot, add in the cumin seeds making sure they crackle. Next, add in the turmeric and cook for about 30 seconds, now straight in with the garlic and ginger and cook these for about another minute.

Now, add in the onions. Cook these until the onions become translucent and then add in the green chillies and cook these for about a minute.

Next, add in the tomatoes and stir into the mixture. Cook this mixture, preferably with the lid on, for 4–5 minutes. After 4–5 minutes, the tomatoes should have softened. Add in the peanuts, salt, and sugar. Next, add in the hot water and stir. Cook for another 5 minutes, add in the garam masala, sprinkle on some fresh coriander, and serve. Done!

> Chef's Tip: The best way to eat this dish is with two wholemeal chapattis. Yumm!

Potato Curry

If you're thinking, *'Potato Curry? How boring!'* you couldn't be more wrong. Believe me, after you have made and eaten this curry, you will be adding this to your top five favourite curries guaranteed! Generally speaking, in India curries are onion based, tomato based, or yoghurt based. The yoghurt-based curries are <u>so</u> tasty that you can take a humble root vegetable like a potato and make it into an *amazingly* tasty curry dish. In fact, the gravy that you will learn to make in this recipe can be applied to lots of other vegetables like cauliflower, cabbage, sweet potato, butternut squash, and the list goes on and on.

Serves 2-3. Prep & Cook time about 20 minutes.

Ingredients:

2 large potatoes parboiled
2 TBSP of vegetable oil
3 TBSP of plain low-fat yoghurt

2 tsp of besan (chickpea flour)
A pinch of hing
1/2 tsp of cumin seeds
1 TBSP of coriander powder
1/2 cup of hot water
1/2 tsp of turmeric
1/2 tsp of deggi mirch
1 TBSP of finely diced red onion
1 tsp of chopped garlic
2–3 chopped green chillies (with or without the seeds—you decide)
A pinch of garam masala
1/2 tsp of brown sugar
A good sprinkle of fresh coriander
Salt to taste

Method:

First, take your two potatoes and parboil them. Cut into large cubes and set aside.

Put the yoghurt in a bowl and add the deggi mirch, turmeric, and coriander powder. Mix really well, ensuring there are no lumps.

Next, place your pan on a medium heat and add the oil; once the oil is hot, add the cumin seeds and the hing and cook these for about 30 seconds, so they release their flavours.

Now add in the garlic and green chilli and fry this for about 1 minute or just until it turns golden brown.

Next, add the besan and stir and toast it in the pan. You will notice that it turns a nutty brown, but be careful not to burn it!

Now, add the yoghurt mixture and turn the heat down slightly—all the while steadily stirring the mixture to ensure the yoghurt does not separate in the pan.

Cook this mixture on a medium heat, stirring continuously, for about 2–3 minutes. After 2–3 minutes, add in some hot water little by little, and never stop stirring.

Add in the potatoes, salt, sugar, and chopped red onion. Cook for another 3 minutes.

Next, remove from the heat and add the fresh coriander and garam masala. Taste it and then tell me if that doesn't taste amazing!

> Chef's Tip: Add a squeeze of fresh lemon just at the end of the cooking process for an off-the-charts taste. ☺

Channa Dal (VV)

Channa dal has a hallowed place in Indian cuisine because the channa (small split chick peas) produce a dal that is like no other in terms of taste, texture, and colour. This dal is very satisfying and hearty. The channa takes longer to cook than red lentils, hence this is another opportunity for me to urge you to buy a pressure cooker, as they make cooking dals easy and, more importantly, quick. This recipe may amaze you as it features only one spice, yet the resulting dal tastes so good, you'll be wondering how that's possible with only the one spice. Okay, there is half a teaspoon of turmeric for colour, but the flavour in this recipe comes essentially from one spice!

Serves 4. Prep & Cook time about 20 minutes.

Ingredients:

1 cup of channa dal
1 H/TBSP of crushed garlic

1/2 tsp of turmeric (for colour)
1 green chilli sliced
1 tsp of cumin seeds
2 ripe tomatoes
1 small onion
Salt to taste
3 TBSP of vegetable oil
1/2 tsp of brown sugar
2 cups of water
1 TBSP of fresh lemon juice

Method:

First, thoroughly wash the channa and soak for one hour before use.

Next, cook the channa in a pressure cooker for about 12–15 minutes. If you're not using a pressure cooker and you're using conventional boiling instead, then you will need to bring them to a boil and simmer for about one and a half hours. Once they are cooked, add about 2 cups of hot water, and set it on the stove on a medium heat. Mash some of the channa with a potato masher. This adds a lovely gelatinous quality to the dal and improves the overall flavour and mouth feel. Set this cooked channa aside in a pan.

Next, take a separate pan for the tarka (spice mixture), add the oil to a pan on a medium heat and, once it's hot, add the cumin seeds. After they crackle, they should start to darken (literally 30 seconds). Add in the turmeric and cook for about 30 seconds more. Be careful that the oil does not smoke. If it does, remove the pan from the heat.

Next, add in garlic and brown slightly, then add in the onion and green chilli and cook for another 30 seconds.

Next, add the tomatoes. Cook these for about 1 minute and then add the contents of this pan to the pan with the channa in it. Stir well then add the salt, sugar, and fresh coriander. Taste and adjust the seasoning.

Next, add in the fresh lemon and stir. The channa shouldn't be too runny or too thick. It should be something in between. If it's too runny then simply cook it for a little longer to reduce the volume and, if it's too thick, add a little boiling water. How easy was that!

> **Chef's Tip:** It is important that the channa is sufficiently cooked. Take one between your thumb and forefinger, and it should squash easily. They should be soft in the mouth not crunchy. ☺

Mung Bean Curried Stew (VV)

I have served this recipe up to friends who don't really like curry (strange folk), and it's always a winner, not just because it tastes great but because I call it 'stew.' If you change the name, their expectations change. This dish is made with mung beans and, to me, these are the tastiest of all the dals. If you're looking for a hearty dish on a cold winter's day, then look no further than this dish, because it's that good. You can eat it on its own without rice or bread.

Serves 3-4. Prep & Cook time about 20 minutes.

Ingredients:

1 cup of dried mung beans
1 medium potato
1 medium carrot
2 medium tomatoes

2 garlic cloves

2 green chillies (Asian variety)

1 inch piece of root ginger

1 tsp of garam masala

1 tsp of cumin seeds

1/2 tsp of turmeric

Salt to taste

1 TBSP of dried curry leaves

2 TBSP of vegetable oil

2 TBSP of lemon Juice

Method:

I recommend soaking the mung beans overnight before use the next day.

Add the soaked mung beans to the pressure cooker and add three times the volume of water. Cook on full pressure for 8 minutes, and they should be done. You will know the beans are cooked because if you take one between your thumb and forefinger it should squash easily. (How easy was that!)

If you're cooking with a conventional pan, then you will need to cook the mung beans for about an hour. Make sure to add three times the volume of water with this method.

Once the beans are cooked, place them in a large pan and add enough water to cover the beans by an inch. Set this pan on a low simmer.

Next, take the peeled potato and cut it into bite-sized chunks. Take the carrot peel it and cut it into fairly thick slices. Take both the potato and carrot and add them to the pan with the mung beans, and then return the pan to a medium heat with the pan lid on but allowing a little gap.

Next, take another pan and add the vegetable oil and heat on a medium heat. Once the oil is hot, add the cumin seeds. They should start to crackle in the oil if the oil is hot enough.

Now, add in the curry leaves and turmeric and fry these for 30 seconds, and then in with the garlic, ginger, chillies, and tomatoes. Stir well in the pan to ensure the garlic doesn't burn. After about 1 minute of cooking, add them to the simmering pan of mung beans and cook this mixture until the potato is cooked.

Once the beans, potato, and carrot all are cooked, add in the salt, garam masala, and lemon juice. Stir. Remove from the heat and leave the mixture to settle for 5 minutes, then serve. It is delicious on its own, with a soft with a soft Naan bread or some short grain brown rice. That's how I have it as shown in the picture.

> Chef's Tip: Just toward the end stage of cooking, before you add in the garam masala and lemon juice, mash some of the mung beans with a potato masher. Add just a little hot water and mix, then in with the lemon, garam masala, and salt, and it will be perfect. ☺

Mixed Vegetable Tikka Masala (VV)

This curry is a big hitter on the taste front, and it's loved by children. My kids loved this when they were young, and, in fact, they still do! This creamy curry is simple and quick to make and is best served with a nice soft naan bread.

Serves 2-3. Prep & Cook time about 15 minutes.

Ingredients:

2 TBSP of vegetable oil
1/2 tsp of turmeric
1 tsp of tandoori masala
1 tsp of garam masala
1/2 tsp of deggi mirch
1/2 tsp of chaat masala
1 tsp of cumin powder

1 tsp of coriander powder

1 TBSP of brown sugar

1 tsp of crushed garlic

Salt to taste

1 large potato cut into small chunks

1 medium carrot cut into chunks

1 cup of frozen peas (defrosted)

1 small red onion rough chopped

1/2 a green pepper cut into large chunks

1/2 a red pepper cut into large chunks

1 tin of crushed tomatoes

1/2 a can of coconut milk

Method:

Take a medium to large pan and heat the oil in the pan.

Next, add in the crushed garlic and fry it just until it starts to turn light brown and then it's straight in with the onion. Fry the onion until it turns translucent. Tip: if it sticks, add a little hot water.

Once the onion has softened, add the turmeric, deggi mirch, coriander, cumin, and tandoori masala. Cook these spices for 1–2 minutes; the aromas will be incredible!

Next, add in all the vegetables, mix these well with all the spices, and cook for 1–2 minutes more.

Next, add a little hot water to loosen everything and cook the vegetables for 3–4 minutes with the lid on the pan.

After 3–4 minutes, remove the lid and add the chaat masala and the garam masala and stir.

Now, add the crushed tomatoes and mix well. Bring all the ingredients in the pan to a simmer and then add the coconut milk, sugar, and salt. Cook the curry, stirring from time to time, until the potato and carrot are cooked. Once these are cooked, remove the pan from the heat and allow the curry to stand for 4–5 minutes, then serve with a nice hot naan bread. Yummy!

> Chef's Tip: Sprinkle a pinch of tandoori masala onto the finished dish just before serving. This will make it look and taste great! ☺

Butter Paneer

This is another example of a dish where you don't need to add many different spices to create something that tastes amazing. This is also an example of a tomato-based curry (remember I mentioned earlier in the book about the three typical bases used in Indian curries: tomato base, yoghurt base, and onion base). This dish is very tasty and has a sumptuous sauce that will keep you coming back for more. This dish is best served with plain boiled rice and a chapatti or two to dip in that delicious sauce. This recipe is dedicated to my son Jacob, because it's his favourite dish and, whenever I make this for him, I can get him to give me a half-hour foot massage. ☺

Serves 4. Prep & Cook time around 20 minutes.

Ingredients:

300 g paneer
2 tins of plum tomatoes blended

5 TBSP of vegetable oil

1 H/TBSP of butter

1 TBSP of garlic paste

1 TBSP of ginger paste

1 H/TBSP of cumin powder

1 tsp of deggi mirch

1 TBSP of garam masala

1 tsp of salt

1 tsp of brown sugar

A handful of fresh coriander

2 TBSP of fresh single cream (18% cream)

Method:

Take a large flat-bottomed pan and heat the oil in the pan over a medium to high heat.

Once the oil is hot, add the butter and melt it. When the butter has melted, add the garlic and ginger paste and fry this for about 1 minute, or until the garlic turns slightly brown.

Next, add in the blended tomatoes and bring this mixture to a vigorous boil. Once boiling, reduce the heat slightly to a simmer and then add the cumin powder. Stir it in well.

Next, add in the deggi mirch and sugar. Mix well and then add the salt and the paneer. Cook the mixture for about 5 minutes. You should start to see the oil separate in the pan.

Next, add in the garam masala, and stir it in well. Cook for just 1–2 minutes more then remove from the heat and add in the single cream. Make sure to mix well. Add in the fresh coriander; taste and adjust the seasoning. Done!

> Chef's Tip: Just before serving, add a swirl of cream. It makes for a great presentation. ☺

Tomato & Potato Curry (VV)

This is another example of a dish with but a few spices—two to be exact. This curry was inspired by a dish I enjoyed at The Chapati Café in Manchester. The reason this dish inspired me was the fact that it was made with *no onions* and, as a result, had a really light and subtle feel on the palate. Hence, I came up with my own version of the recipe. As I've mentioned a few times already in this book, curries in India are generally from one of three bases: onion, yoghurt, or tomato. This curry has a tomato base and it works so well with the humble potato (or spud as we say in Lancashire).

Serves 3-4. Prep & Cook time about 25 minutes.

Ingredients:

2 TBSP of vegetable oil

1/2 a lb (225 g) of peeled, pre-cooked, and diced potatoes

1/2 a lb (225 g) of chopped tomatoes

1 tsp of ginger paste
1 TBSP of garlic paste
1 tsp of black mustard seeds
1 tsp of cumin seeds
1/2 tsp of deggi mirch
1 TBSP of fresh coriander
1/2 tsp of sugar
Salt to taste
1 cup of hot water

Method:

Heat the oil in a wide-bottomed pan.

Once the oil is hot, add in the black mustard. When they start to pop, add in the cumin seeds and wait for them to crackle.

Next, add in the ginger and garlic and cook for one minute or until the garlic begins to turn brown.

Now, add in the deggi mirch and the fresh coriander and stir it in.

Add in the tomatoes, salt, sugar, and hot water and cook for about 10 minutes on medium to high heat. Stir occasionally.

After 10 minutes or so, the tomatoes should have broken down. Remove from the heat and allow to cool for 10 minutes.

Once the mixture has cooled, take a stick blender and blend the mixture until smooth. Add the mixture back into the pan and add in the potatoes. Return to the heat and cook for a further 5 minutes. If the mixture is a little too thick, add a little bit more hot water. What we are aiming for is a gravy, not a thick sauce.

Julian Voigt

Taste and adjust seasoning. Done!

> Chef's Tip: Add some additional fresh coriander before serving. Don't serve this dish too hot. Allow it to stand for 3-4 minutes before you serve, and it will taste better. ☺

Split Mung Dal with Spinach (VV)

If you follow me on YouTube, you may have seen a video review I did of a fantastic little eatery in Chorlton Manchester at The Chapati Café. The food there is extraordinary as are the owners Dan and Priti. They have worked with a lot of passion to create an eatery that serves up authentic Indian food at its best.

There are very few restaurants that you come across these days where the food served has an element of the heart and soul imparted into the food by the owners and chefs. In my opinion, this place has it!

When I visited there, I tried a vegetarian thali and one of the dishes on that thali was their famous 'Split Mung Dal & Spinach' as recommended by co-owner Dan. I can only describe this dish as amazing. The flavour was *so* good I had to get the recipe from Dan & Priti. Thankfully, they very kindly gave it to me. I asked them if they would mind if I shared this with my readers, and they were happy for me to do that, hence, it's the final recipe in the book.

Now this recipe breaks the rules because the preparation and cook time for this recipe is about 45 minutes. So, unlike all the other recipes in this book, it doesn't exactly fit the quick theme. But I think you will agree after you have made and eaten this incredible dish that the extra time it takes to make it is more than worth it, and you'll be glad that Dan & Priti were happy to share their trade secrets of one of their top-selling recipes with us. So, thanks to Dan & Priti. ☺

You can see the video I made about Chapati Café here with details under the video as to how to find them:

VIDEO: https://www.youtube.com/edit?o=U&video_id=tzqUjMW9urg

Serves 4. Prep & Cook Time about 45 minutes.

Ingredients:

1 cup of split mung beans (soaked 30 minutes before use)
1-1/2 chef spoons of vegetable oil
A scant TBSP of cumin seeds
2 medium white onions finely sliced
Half of a 400 g can of chopped tomatoes
6 fresh tomatoes chopped roughly
A scant TBSP of black mustard seeds
1 scant TBSP salt
1 tsp of turmeric
1 TBSP cumin powder
1-1/2 TBSP coriander powder
4 cloves of garlic crushed into paste
1 inch piece of ginger paste

1 tsp of chilli powder

1 tsp of ground black pepper

2 bay leaves

1 TBSP tamarind concentrate (small Natco bottles are best)

1 teaspoon sugar

Handful of chopped fresh coriander

Pinch of curry leaves

2 green chillies split into halves

1/4 tsp hing

1 bunch spinach (from Asian grocers)

Method:

Heat oil over medium to high heat in the pan.

Once the oil is hot, add in the black mustard seeds and wait for them to pop (don't forget to dodge those burning missiles ☺).

Now, add in the cumin seeds and the green chillies and wait for the sizzle.

Next, it's in with the curry leaves and stir.

Now, add in the hing.

Next, add in the onions, salt, and bay leaves. Cover the pan and allow them to cook over a medium heat.

After about 15 minutes, the onions should have turned a deep brown colour and have become sticky. (***It's important to the flavour of this dish that you wait till this has happened.***)

When the onions are done, add in the garlic and ginger and mix well.

Next, add in the powdered spices: turmeric, cumin, coriander, chilli powder, and black pepper. Stir in and cook those spices for 1-2 minutes.

Now we add in the tinned and fresh tomatoes.

Cook everything together now for about 15 minutes or until the oil starts to separate.

Once the oil has separated, add in the pre-cooked split mung dal along with the water they were boiled in and stir.

Next, add in the sugar and tamarind. If needed, add a little more hot water.

Stir the mixture well and leave everything to cook for a further 15 minutes but check and stir occasionally.

After 15 minutes, it should be done. Remove from the heat, add the fresh coriander, and serve.

> Chef's Tip: When I had this, I had it with plain rice, a chapatti, and a nice little cabbage, carrot, and coriander salad. It was AMAZING! ☺

So, that's the recipes, but some final advice . . .

There's a saying that the better we are at doing something the more enjoyable it becomes, and the more likely we are to do it.

I think we all relate to the truth of that saying. I have found that some people fret when they are called on to make a meatless meal. Generally, that's because it challenges their paradigm. I hope that the recipes in this book inspire you to become an excellent vegetarian curry cook. In my humble opinion, the best curry cooks are those who can take some humble ingredients like chickpeas or potatoes and make them into something quite spectacular. I believe the dishes I have included in this book fall into that category.

I always remember being impressed at a very young age by authentic vegetarian Indian cuisine. I had never before come across such variety and flavours and, after experiencing the delights of this cuisine, I was left feeling that, by comparison, all other foods were bland and uninspiring. I honestly believe that South Asian cuisine is not only the tastiest in the world, but also the most varied.

I think the reason Indian people, who are vegetarians, are able to make dishes from humble vegetables taste *so good* is simply how they view vegetables. For example, some of us look at vegetables in the Western world as a garnish or an accompaniment to the main meal—the meat. So, to put it another way, the Indian community exalt the foods we often view as a side dish.

I think if we can adopt their view, then we will start to view these humble vegetables as the main attraction and, from such a changed perspective, we will go on to create the very best of vegetable-based dishes.

'Quality Counts'

This might sound like an obvious statement to make but how many times have we bit into a piece of fruit or eaten a vegetable that was tasteless? 'All too often!' I hear you say. We have to become better at choosing produce that might not look appealing but will certainly taste appealing. Often we are sold on appearance rather than quality, and we shouldn't confuse the two.

In the modern world, fruits and vegetables are produced with almost factory-like efficiency for the big supermarket chains. Sadly however, their priority is profit and that means shelf life. Hence produce is picked when unripe and thus lacking most of the nutrients that would have normally been present in that vegetable had it been allowed to ripen on the tree, vine, or plant. How often have you eaten tomatoes that didn't taste like tomatoes? Or eaten potatoes that are watery with no flavour?

Why do I mention all of this? Because I would encourage you to look for local produce. Find out when the next local Farmer's Market is or shop at the smaller grocers stores that buy their produce locally. The produce may not look as 'perfect' as the stuff you come across in the big supermarkets, but I'm sure you'll find that it tastes a lot better.

You should also try the Asian stores where you find your spices. Often, the produce there is a better quality. Don't be put off if the bell pepper has an odd shape or has a few wrinkles; chances are it tastes so much better than the perfect plastic-looking stuff you find in the big chain supermarkets.

Fresh Spices

Invest in your spice cupboard. Having a well-stocked spice cupboard ensures you will always be able to rustle up a tasty dish. Keep those spices in airtight containers away from sunlight, so they will last longer. If possible, grind your own cumin and coriander powder—*this little bit of extra effort makes a <u>huge</u> difference!*

Make your own garam masala—again, this is another thing that will take your dishes to another level.

Deggi mirch—I have exclusively used this over regular chilli powder in all the recipes in this book. I did this because the taste and quality is superior and this small improvement goes a long way to make the finished dish something out of the ordinary. If you can't find it, make your own. It's quite simple. Simply buy some Kashmiri type chillies (the long dark red variety), remove the seeds, grind them up, and you will have deggi mirch. Or, if you can't do that for whatever reason then take regular chilli powder and mix it 50/50 with a good quality paprika and you will have something that resembles deggi mirch.

Buy your spices in bulk. This will not only save you money in the long run, but it will also ensure you never run out. Buy good quality brands like Rajah or East End. TRS spices are also good. Natco is another good brand.

Experiment

Never be afraid to experiment. This is how great dishes come into being. In my own personal experience, some of the best dishes I have cooked have been when I accidently left *something out*. Often, we think in terms of *adding* more, but why not try leaving something out and see if it improves the dish? Don't get me wrong. I'm not suggesting you sabotage the recipes in this book but get creative and see what YOU can come up with.

***

I hope you enjoy the recipes in this book, and please feel free to contact me through my website: www.curryrecipesectrets.com and let me know if you come up with a masterpiece. Who knows, I might feature it on my YouTube channel or it might end up in a future book with due credit given to yourself of course!

I want to take this opportunity to thank you for buying this book and for allowing me to fulfil my passion by sharing what I have learned about what I unashamedly describe as the world's tastiest food. Hopefully, we may get a chance to connect in the future—maybe through one of our cooking courses both on and offline.

Wishing you happiness and health!

Julian Voigt

About the Author

If you enjoyed this book maybe you'd enjoy these other books by the same author:

The Secret to That Takeaway Curry Taste

Julian reveals the closely guarded secrets of the British Indian restaurant trade and shows you how easy it is. Once you have done some core preparations to make your favourite Indian restaurant or takeaway curry in around 10 minutes, the amazing thing is that it will taste EXACTLY like the Indian restaurant or takeaway curry. This book is available from this website: www.curryrecipesecrets.com as an eBook. For the printed version, you can get it here on Amazon: http://amzn.to/1LVtIuZ .

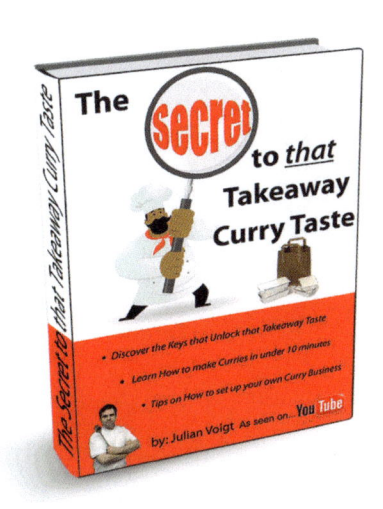

Get it here: http://bit.ly/1LeZys7

The Secret to That Takeaway Curry Taste-Part 2

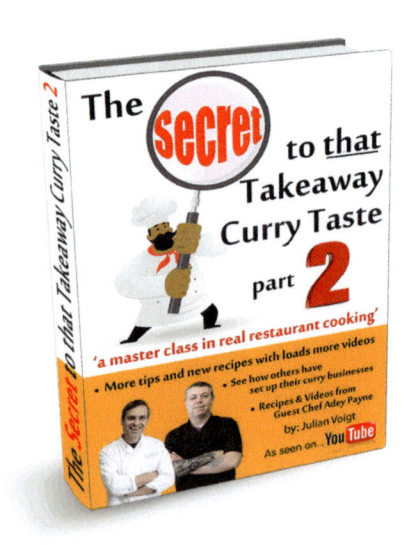

Get it here: http://bit.ly/1LeZys7

The story continues—one of Julian's students, Adey, took what he learned and opened his own Indian takeaway restaurant and went on to get voted No. 1 on the Trip Advisor in the Boston area for Indian food. Together, Julian and Adey share loads more insights, know-how, and, of course, recipes to help you master British Indian restaurant cuisine. This book comes with links to over 27 video tutorials.

Would you like to take your curry cooking skills to the next level? Would you like to have Julian and Adey show you how to master curry cooking and produce curries and other dishes that your friends and family wow over? Have you always fancied attending a cooking school but couldn't find one local to you? Would you love to attend a course but haven't got the time with your busy schedule?

Then we might have just what you've been looking for!

Starting in December 2015, Julian, Adey, and his team are opening an online curry cooking academy.

This online cooking academy will take you behind the scenes of Julian and Adey's British Indian Restaurant Cooking Academy in Alford, Lincolnshire, in the UK where you will see professionally edited video footage of their cooking school run at Adey's restaurant, **Fusion Indian Restaurant**. You will be able to enjoy the online version of this cooking course that teaches courses in the following:

'British Indian Restaurant Curry Secrets Revealed'

'Authentic Homestyle Indian Curry Secrets Revealed'

'Authentic Vegetarian Indian Curry Secrets Revealed'

'Master the Tandoori Oven'

In these online courses, you will learn everything the students who attend these courses learn.

You can choose one or all courses on our new membership site starting December 2015.

Why not allow Julian and Adey to share with you their curry cooking skills and knowledge.

Check out what the students have said who have taken their courses: **http://bit.ly/1QHb11v**

*** SPECIAL OFFER ***

As a thank you for buying this book, you can claim your 30% discount off any of our online courses. Simply email Julian here: julianvoigt_23@hotmail.com with this coupon code:

QECR/COUPON30 and this will entitle you to a whopping 30% off any of Julian and Adey's online cooking courses.

For more information about these online courses, visit: www.curryrecipeacademy.com.

Printed in Great Britain
by Amazon